THE BEST OF
ROCKY MOUNTAIN
NATIONAL PARK

by ALAN LEFTRIDGE

View from Chasm Lake, NPS photo, John Marino

THE BEST OF
ROCKY MOUNTAIN
NATIONAL PARK

by ALAN LEFTRIDGE

ACKNOWLEDGMENTS

Thank you to Linda, who shares my life and is a co-contributor to the content and spirit of this book. She read every draft and her suggestions improved the overall clarity of the writing.

I also want to acknowledge Katy Sykes who reviewed several sections and provided photos from the RMNP archive, and Cynthia Langguth who helped with the alpine tundra and plants sections. The bird section was reviewed by Richard Gilliland, a park volunteer who leads bird walks.

"The Best of" series is edited by Will Harmon at Farcountry Press. I am pleased to work with Will and am grateful for his precise editing and enthusiasm for the art of interpretive writing.

ISBN: 978-1-56037-635-4

© 2015 by Farcountry Press
Text © 2015 by Alan Leftridge

Cover photograph © Thomas Mangan.
Inset cover photography courtesy National Park Service.

All rights reserved. This book may not be reproduced in whole or in part by any means (with the exception of short quotes for the purpose of review) without the permission of the publisher.

For more information about our books, write Farcountry Press, P.O. Box 5630, Helena, MT 59604; call (800) 821-3874; or visit www.farcountrypress.com.

Cataloging-in-Publication data on file at the Library of Congress.

 Produced and printed in the United States of America.

19 18 17 16 15   1 2 3 4 5 6

Preface .... *xi*

How to Use the Maps in This Book .... *xii*

Rocky Mountain National Park's Legacy. *1*

Where's Rocky? *2*

Rocky: Just the Facts. *3*

Rocky's Weather. *4*

Ten Things You May Not Know About Rocky *6*

**A Short Cultural History of
Rocky Mountain National Park** *7*

Best Historic Sites. *9*

    1. Holzwarth Historic District. 10

    2. Lulu City. 10

    3. Moraine Park Discovery Center 11

    4. Beaver Meadows Visitor Center. 11

    5. Old Fall River Road. 12

CCC in Rocky. *13*

Notable People of Rocky *14*

    Earl of Dunraven. 14

    Isabella Bird 14

    James Nugent 14

    Joel Estes 14

    Abner Sprague. 15

    William Henry Jackson 15

    James Grafton Rogers 16

    John Holzwarth Sr. 16

    Freelan Oscar Stanley 16

    Enos Mills. 17

    Esther Burnell. 18

Rocky's Artist-in-Residence Program *19*
Best Visitor Centers. *20*
    1. Beaver Meadows Visitor Center. 21
    2. Moraine Park Visitor Center 21
    3. Fall River Visitor Center 21
    4. Kawuneeche Visitor Center. 22
    5. Alpine Visitor Center. 22
Rocky's Shuttle: Leave the Driving to Us. *23*
Best Scenic Drives. *24*
    1. Bear Lake Road. 24
    2. Fall River Road 27
    3. Trail Ridge Road. 29
Best Picnic Areas. *34*
    1. Hidden Valley 34
    2. Sprague Lake 35
    3. Lily Lake. 35
    4. Lake Irene. 36
    5. Coyote Valley. 36
Best Horseback Rides. *38*
Best Names of Natural Features *39*
A Concise History of Rocky's Geology. *41*
Tundra Rock Art: The Lichens *42*
Best Self-Guided Trails. *43*
    1. Tundra Communities Trail 43
    2. Bear Lake Nature Trail. 44
    3. Colorado River Trail (Lulu City). 45
    4. Coyote Valley Trail 45

    5. Lily Lake Trail. 46

    6. Sprague Lake Nature Trail 46

Visiting Bear Country **47**

Hiking in Rocky. **49**

Best Day Hikes **50**

    1. Bear, Nymph, Dream, and Emerald Lakes 50

    2. Bierstadt Lake 51

    3. Lake Haiyaha 52

    4. The Loch 53

    5. Cub Lake. 53

    6. Ouzel Lake 54

    7. Gem Lake 55

    8. Ute Trail 55

Best Waterfalls **57**

    1. Bridal Veil Falls 57

    2. Fern Falls 58

    3. Alberta Falls 59

    4. Copeland Falls. 59

    5. Ouzel Falls. 60

    6. Adams Falls. 60

    7. Cascade Falls. 61

Best Fish **62**

    Greenback Cutthroat Trout. 62

    Colorado River Cutthroat Trout 62

    Brown Trout 63

    Rainbow Trout 63

    Brook Trout. 63

Best Fishing ... 64
Best Lake Fishing ... 64
Best Stream Fishing ... 64

Best Birds ... 65
Broad-tailed hummingbird ... 65
Ruby-crowned Kinglet ... 65
Pygmy Nuthatch ... 66
Black-capped Chickadee ... 66
Mountain Chickadee ... 67
American Dipper ... 68
Western Tanager ... 68
Steller's Jay ... 69
Gray Jay ... 69
Clark's Nutcracker ... 70
Black-billed Magpie ... 70
Northern Flicker ... 71
Red-naped Sapsucker ... 71
White-tailed Ptarmigan ... 72
American Kestrel ... 72
Golden Eagle ... 73

Best Mammals ... 74
Chipmunks ... 74
Golden-mantled Ground Squirrel ... 74
Wyoming Ground Squirrel ... 75
Red Squirrel ... 76
Pika ... 77
Snowshoe Hare ... 78

Yellow-bellied Marmot 78

Bighorn Sheep. 79

Mule Deer. 80

Elk. 81

Moose 82

Coyote. 83

Black Bear. 84

Mountain Lion 85

Best Places to See Wildlife from the Road **86**

Notable Insects. **88**

A Superabundance of Butterflies. 88

Other Insects. 90

Best Wildflowers. **92**

Alpine Avens 93

Snow-lily 93

Alpine Sunflower. 94

Heartleaf Arnica 94

Colorado Columbine. 95

Alpine Forget-me-not 95

Pasqueflower 96

Sky Pilot 96

Mountain Harebell 97

Mountain Lupine 97

Fairy Slipper 98

Fireweed 98

Shooting Star. 99

Paintbrush. 99

Best Trees **101**
    Ponderosa Pine 101
    Lodgepole Pine 102
    Limber Pine 103
    Engelmann Spruce 103
    Colorado Blue Spruce 104
    Subalpine Fir... 104
    Douglas-fir 104
    Quaking Aspen 106

Best Activities for Children........................... **107**
Best Things to Do on a Rainy or Snowy Summer's Day... **112**
Winter in Rocky **113**
Best Sunrise and Sunset Spots.......................... **115**
Iconic Subjects to Photograph **116**
Best Places to Take a Personal Portrait................ **117**
Best Books About Rocky................................. **118**
Resources **121**
About the Author **124**

PREFACE

"What is there to do?" is a question that you might ask of a park employee or a friend familiar with the park. But you may have neither person to ask as you schedule your vacation. With limited time, it is best to plan your visit so that you are able to take in the locations that others have found most symbolic of the park.

The purpose of this book is to enhance your visit by sharing some of the linkages of the cultural heritage and natural history of Rocky Mountain National Park. I will point out the iconic features and relate to you the best of the park as identified by some of the people who work and live here. This book shares with you what I think you should know about the park, as if you were a family member or friend visiting for the first time.

I'll encourage you to experience new connections with the land. I want you to recognize some of the adaptations that plants and animals have for living in this wild, untamed place. I'll also give you ideas about how to best share your experiences with family and friends.

This book is intended to inspire you to discover the wonder of life and its adaptive diversity in Rocky Mountain National Park, through your interests in sightseeing, hiking, wildlife viewing, wildflower admiration, photographing, and learning its natural and cultural history. These stories and experiences will lead you to the essence of Rocky Mountain National Park—*The Backbone of the Continent*.

Alan Leftridge

HOW TO USE THE MAPS IN THIS BOOK

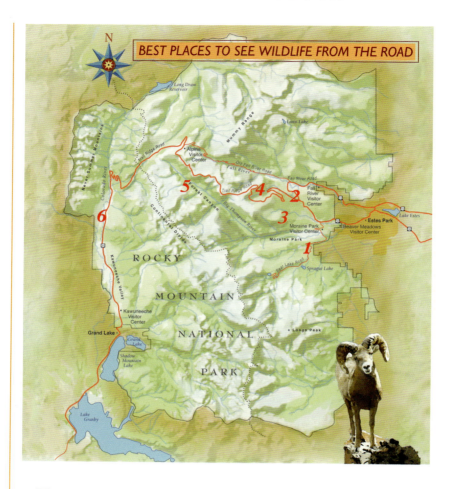

The maps in this book show numbered locations for features and activities described in each chapter. Some indicate general areas, while others show more specific locations for individual subjects explained in the text. Use these maps with the more detailed visitor map you receive at any entrance station. For hiking, backpacking, and climbing, more detailed topographic maps are recommended, available at vendors in communities around the park.

ROCKY MOUNTAIN NATIONAL PARK'S LEGACY

You may have already experienced a crisp night atop Trail Ridge Road when the Milky Way seemed close enough to touch, or marveled at the rising sun burnishing Rocky's alpine tundra in radiant splendor —or maybe shared a barefoot romp across a snowfield in July. Rocky Mountain National Park boasts a high percentage of return visitors. In fact, generations of people have always gathered in the park seeking experiences, building memories, and sharing their stories with family and friends. This is Rocky Mountain National Park's legacy.

Progressive-minded people wanted to preserve this landscape for future generations. Their efforts and your stories will continue to inspire friends and family members to visit and return to encounter the wonders of Rocky Mountain National Park—discoveries that will span lifetimes.

WHERE'S ROCKY?

Look at the park map that you received at the entrance station. Notice that the park boundaries are straight lines in some places and zigzag, following mountain ridges, in others. Enos Mills, the "father" of Rocky Mountain National Park, wanted a 1-million-acre park; Congress approved an area one-fourth that size. The park's borders are concessions to administrative concerns.

Consider the distribution of Rocky's fauna and flora. The Colorado columbine blooms throughout the region, not just in the park. In winter, elk are drawn to lower elevations beyond park boundaries. Mountain lions and black bears are found where their habitats provide ample forage and cover, freely wandering between the park and the surrounding national forests. Neither plants nor animals are adapted to boundaries drawn on a map.

So, where's Rocky? It is at the heart of a greater landscape in the Southern Rocky Mountains. It is politically unbounded by the flora and fauna that live here. The park is a multifaceted, intertwining organization of plants, animals, and humans, connected by the landscape and the streams—life-giving sustenance—that flow east and west from Rocky's backbone, the Continental Divide.

> **WHAT IS A PARK?**
>
> The word "park" has several meanings. The American Heritage Dictionary lists 10 nuances. How does the word apply here?
>
> Rocky Mountain National Park is an area of land kept in its natural state for public recreational use.
>
> Moraine Park is a broad, flat, open pocket of land in a mountainous region.
>
> Estes Park is a broad, flat, open pocket of land in a mountainous region, and also the name of the town located in that park.

ROCKY: JUST THE FACTS

- President Woodrow Wilson signed the legislation that established Rocky as the tenth national park on January 26, 1915.
- The park covers 415 square miles or 265,761 acres.
- The highest point in the park is Longs Peak at 14,259 feet above sea level. The lowest elevation is 7,860 feet.
- The park has more than 60 peaks over 12,000 feet.
- Treeline in the park is at approximately 11,500 feet; more than one-third of the park is above this height.
- There are about 355 miles of hiking trails.
- The park has 147 named lakes and 473 miles of streams.
- Wildlife species includes 66 mammals, 280 birds, 5 amphibians, and 1 reptile (a garter snake).
- The National Park Service estimates more than 1,000 species of flowering plants live in Rocky.
- Rocky Mountain National Park holds the headwaters of the Colorado, Big Thompson, Cache la Poudre, and Fall Rivers.
- Annual visitation exceeds 3 million, with July the busiest month and March the quietest.
- Rocky Mountain National Park is open 24 hours a day, every day of the year (some roads close in winter).

ROCKY'S WEATHER

Storm over Lumpy Ridge, NPS photo, Ann Schonlau

What kind of weather should you expect when you come to Rocky? That depends, of course, on the season of your visit. Keep in mind that most of Rocky is a high-elevation alpine park. Winter-like weather can happen year-round!

If you are visiting during summer, be prepared for mild days with temperatures reaching the 80s, and cool nights into the 40s. Afternoon thunderstorms can produce lightning, hail, and high winds. Many of these thunderstorms are convection-type, which build with little notice and produce violent weather. A cloudless morning can turn to an unsettled afternoon with little notice.

You may want to visit during autumn, when the weather is relatively dry, with cool, cloudless days and crisp, starlit nights. Aspen leaves turn to liquid gold, and the bugling of bull elk echoes from the mountainsides. Expect high temperatures in the 50s and nighttime lows in the 30s. Wet snow can begin falling by mid-October, so expect Trail Ridge Road to close, but touring Bear Lake Road can be a highlight of your holiday.

Visitation during winter drops to the annual low, and so do the temperatures. The tundra experiences -35°F temperatures with blizzard conditions and deep snowpack in downwind areas. High elevations can pile several feet of snow, while low-lying valleys may accumulate only a few inches. The park west of the Continental Divide typically receives a lot of snow, while the eastern side of the divide gets less precipitation.

Springtime is a long transitional season where snow lingers into May in the alpine areas, while the montane meadows host an explosion of wildflowers. Typical of the southern Rockies, snowfall occurs into April, as the weather patterns remain unpredictable. You will experience alternating warm and cool, wet and dry days. Trail Ridge Road opens in late May, so expect an increasing number of fellow travelers as the season progresses.

Regardless of the time of year, you will discover that the weather adds enjoyment to your visit. Return each season to experience the seasonal changes that you will see in Rocky's plants and animals.

CLIMATE CHANGE IN ROCKY

Plant and animal populations adapt to climatic changes. There are enough variations in most gene pools to respond to external pressures, over time. But unnatural disruptions in the earth's climate have accelerated since the Industrial Revolution. Many plant and animal gene pools cannot keep pace with the speed of changes in their habitats.

Evidence of environmental changes in Rocky Mountain National Park is broad. The winter snowpack is melting up to two weeks earlier than historic records document, meaning less water is available for people, plants, and animals during summer. Warmer

Measuring Andrews Glacier, NPS archives

winter months have resulted in an explosive infestation of pine beetles, evidenced by dying and dead trees throughout the park. Earlier-than-normal spring weather means that some wildflowers bloom before their pollinators arrive. Pika populations are at increasing risk as more days climb above 75°F, the ceiling where pikas can survive. Plants and animals adapted for other climates are invading all of Rocky's life zones, outcompeting native species, and disrupting the park's delicate balance.

The rapidity of these changes puts Rocky at risk. If wildfires increase, water runoff diminishes, and invasive species continue to displace the iconic plants and animals that we treasure, Rocky will lose its identity. How should we respond? Become educated to the facts gathered by science academies worldwide. Hold our decision-makers responsible for making wise choices to ensure that Rocky will continue to meet the mandate of the National Park Service: **to conserve the scenery and the natural and historic objects and the wild life therein and to provide for the enjoyment of the same in such manner and by such means as will leave them unimpaired for the enjoyment of future generations.**

TEN THINGS YOU MAY NOT KNOW ABOUT ROCKY

- One early proposed name for the park was Estes National Park. Robert Sterling Yard, Chief of Education for the National Park Service, wanted the park to span three large sections that included Pikes Peak. The U.S. Geological Survey offered a more inclusive name for the backbone of the Rocky Mountains, and even though Yard's dream was not realized, the newer name stuck.

- Enos Mills (the "father" of Rocky Mountain National Park) made an original proposal for park boundaries that stretched from Wyoming to Mount Evans, including areas such as the Indian Peaks Wilderness and Central City.

- There are no poisonous snakes in the park, and the garter snake is the only reptile.

- Two-thirds of the annual visitors have been to the park more than five times.

- Major Stephen H. Long led a government scientific expedition to the Rocky Mountain front in 1820. Although the group did not enter the mountains, Longs Peak was named in his honor.

- Ninety-eight percent of the park is designated wilderness.

- Red squirrels *(Tamiasciurus hudsonicus)*, common in Rocky, are not red. Instead, they are gray with white stomachs. Here they are called pine squirrels or chickarees.

- The Cache la Poudre River, with its headwaters in Rocky Mountain National Park, is designated a Wild River within the National Wild and Scenic Rivers System. From the park, it flows through the Arapaho and Roosevelt National Forests, through both the Comanche Peak and Cache la Poudre Wilderness Areas. When it exits Cache la Poudre Canyon, it is a part of the Cache la Poudre River National Heritage Area. No other river in the United States has so many designations.

- Almost 800 elk winter in the park.

- There are 141 documented species of butterflies that inhabit the park.

A SHORT CULTURAL HISTORY OF ROCKY MOUNTAIN NATIONAL PARK

The Estes Park area before settlement, William Henry Jackson, courtesy of U.S. Geological Survey

The history of the Rocky Mountain National Park area is marked by discovery and adaptation to the environment.

Paleo-Indian groups wandered the region as far back as 10,000 years, but left little trace. The Ute and Arapaho people are the first identifiable groups to inhabit parts of the area. The Ute tribe lived west of the Continental Divide, venturing east to hunt bison. East of the divide, Arapaho visited the Estes Park area. Neither tribe claimed permanent residence. Both groups withdrew from the area when Euro-Americans pushed into the central Rocky Mountains.

Major Stephen Long explored eastern Colorado on a government expedition in 1820. He did not venture into the mountains but recorded seeing Longs Peak. It was later named in his honor.

While on a deer hunting trip in the fall of 1843, Rufus Sage was the first Euro-American to visit the Estes Park area. His stay was brief.

Joel Estes found the area that bears his name in 1859. His family was the first to settle and begin cattle ranching. Others followed, taking advantage of the 1862 Homestead Act. Coincidentally, gold was discovered in the Denver area and, soon after, in and around present-day Rocky Mountain National Park. Neither ranching nor mining proved profitable.

In the late 1800s, an increasing number of adventure-minded tourists sought provisions and information from landowners. Ranch owners realized that the visitors were willing to pay high prices for services.

Enos Mills, F. O. Stanley (holding flag), and others, dedication ceremony, NPS photo

Many of the homesteads were converted to profitable guest ranches.

Other people were attracted to the region for health. Isabella Bird, F. O. Stanley, and Enos Mills were encouraged to stay because the clean mountain air was thought to be "healthy." They each, in their own way, promoted the preservation of the area. Their efforts were rewarded in 1915 when President Woodrow Wilson signed legislation to establish Rocky Mountain National Park.

BEST HISTORIC SITES

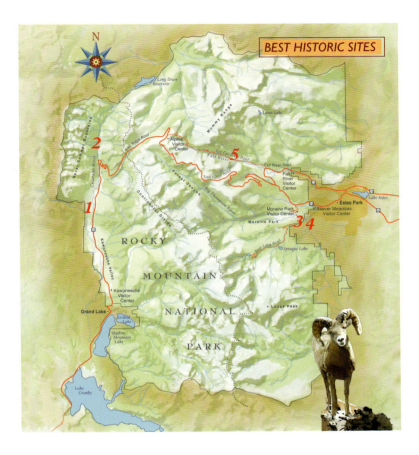

Archaeological evidence suggests that people roamed these mountains 10,000 years ago, leaving little trace. American Indians who knew this area included the Utes and Arapaho. The Utes frequented the Grand Lake vicinity and occasionally came across the Continental Divide to hunt bison on the plains. The Arapaho were plains Indians and came to the Estes Park area in the summer to hunt.

The Euro-Americans came to settle, and left their marks on the land. Many of their buildings have been eradicated, by nature or National Park Service policies. There remain dozens of structures, roads, and trails listed on the National Register of Historic Places. The most interesting sites are Holzwarth Ranch, Lulu City, Moraine Park Lodge, Beaver Meadows Visitor Center, and Old Fall River Road. Visit them all!

1. Holzwarth Historic District

Saloon owner John Holzwarth was forced to close his business with the enactment of Prohibition in 1919. Turning to a rancher's life, he relocated his family to the Kawuneeche Valley and founded the Never Summer Ranch. That did not work out either, as making a living raising cattle in the harsh climate and remote area was difficult. Holzwarth learned, however, that vacationers were happy to pay top dollar for meals, accommodations, supplies, and entertainment. He converted his operation to a dude ranch, named it Holzwarth Trout Lodge, and prospered. Today, you can visit the site and see several buildings. The National Park Service maintains the homestead cabin, and volunteers share what it was like to visit a 1920s dude ranch.

The Holzwarth Ranch in 1973, NPS archives

2. Lulu City

Prospector Joe Shipler announced his find of silver near the headwaters of the Colorado River in 1879, and the rush for riches began. Fort Collins entrepreneur Benjamin F. Burnett helped finance the development of a town and named it for his daughter. The city was laid out on an ambitious scale—100 city blocks were planned. The town boomed, growing to almost 200 residents, with 40 houses, 2 sawmills, a general store, a mining supply store, a grocery store, a barbershop, a clothing store, a hotel, a restaurant, and an assay office. Unfortunately for the residents, the assay officers determined that the silver ore was of low grade. Also, high transportation costs from this remote locale meant that mining profits were marginal at best.

Remnants of Lulu City, NPS archives

Dreams of wealth faded and the town was abandoned by 1885, except for one resident, the first prospector, Joe Shipler, who stayed for the next 30 years. Explore the area of Lulu City; 3 cabin ruins, some foundations, and various other remnants remain. Look over the grassy area next to the Colorado River and imagine a town expected to be the size of 100 city blocks.

Moraine Park Discovery Center, NPS archives

3. Moraine Park Discovery Center

Several lodges operated in Rocky Mountain Park during its early years, including those at Sprague Lake, Horseshoe Park, and Bear Lake. The Moraine Park Lodge was built in 1923 and included several cabins and outbuildings. The Moraine Park Discovery Center once housed the lodge's dance hall and tearoom. The National Park Service acquired the property in 1931, removed the outbuildings, and converted the dance hall to the Moraine Park Visitor Center. It opened to the public in 1937. You will find exhibits featuring the major themes of the park, including geologic processes, climate, ecosystems, and human impact.

4. Beaver Meadows Visitor Center

Famed architect Frank Lloyd Wright founded the Taliesin Associated Architects firm to carry on his design visions after his death. The group was commissioned to design the Beaver Meadows Visitor Center for Mission 66, an initiative to upgrade infrastructure in national parks across the country. The steel and stone building was completed in 1967 and was designated a National Historic Landmark

Beaver Meadows Visitor Center, NPS archives

in 2001. Today, it also houses Rocky's administration offices. Stop at the Beaver Meadows Visitor Center to view a park orientation film and enjoy the beauty of the building's design. Information about the park, activities, maps, and books are available.

5. Old Fall River Road

This one-way dirt road was originally designed for travel in both directions as the first highway to cross this part of the Rocky Mountains. Begun in 1913, it was completed in 1920 and connected Horseshoe Park with Grand Lake. Soon after its completion, construction began on Trail Ridge Road. Fall River Road was soon limited to one-way traffic, east to west. A slide closed it in 1953, and the National Park Service made only limited repairs. It remained unavailable to visitor traffic until an upwelling of popular support encouraged the park service to fix the road. It reopened in 1968. Drive Fall River Road to discover how visitors saw the park in its early years.

Old Fall River Road, NPS photo, Ann Schonlau

CCC IN ROCKY

CCC workers in Rocky, NPS archives

Black Thursday, October 24, 1929, struck the nation like a lightning bolt, as the stock market crashed. Unemployment reached 25 percent by 1933. President Franklin Roosevelt responded by initiating several programs to pull the country from depression. The Civilian Conservation Corps (CCC) was formed in 1933 to help revive the economy. Men between 17 and 28 were employed to build the nation's rural infrastructure and reclaim despoiled landscapes. For the next 9 years, CCC members worked from camps on projects to preserve America's natural and historical heritage.

Five camps operated in and one adjacent to Rocky Mountain National Park. One camp was at Little Horseshoe Park, two camps were near Beaver Creek, and two others at Mill Creek. At Grand Lake, a sixth camp focused on projects within the park.

The camps operated between May 1933 and July 1942. Hundreds of CCC members constructed bridges, buildings, trails, amphitheaters, reservoirs, fishponds, and rock walls within the park. They also fought forest fires, conducted search and rescue missions, laid utility lines, landscaped, reforested disturbed areas, and maintained trails. The camps were long ago obliterated, but the legacy of the CCC in Rocky Mountain National Park can be found in the infrastructure improvements that Corps members accomplished.

NOTABLE PEOPLE OF ROCKY

Earl of Dunraven
His name was Windham Thomas Wyndham-Quinn, the 4th Earl of Dunraven.

The Earl had a reputed passion for beautiful women, fine wines, horse racing, and big game hunting. He arrived in Estes Park in 1872 and found the hunting fabulous.

The following year he returned and began buying all available land in Estes Park. Was it for cattle ranching or making a private hunting preserve? No one knows. He then built the Estes Park Hotel and opened it for guests in 1877.

Squabbles accelerated with settlers adjacent to his 8,000-acre holdings, as the Earl used aggressive methods to force them to sell to him.

There are questions about his motives for buying much of Estes Park, and it is uncertain why he left in the mid-1880s. What is true is that his ownership ensured that a large parcel of land was kept from development. He retained ownership of most of his holdings until 1908, when he sold everything to B. D. Sanborn and F. O. Stanley.

Isabella Bird
Isabella's life of traveling began in 1854 when she sailed to America from England. Her bright descriptive letters home were printed in a popular European magazine, establishing her as a travel writer. She discovered that the Colorado air was considered healthful, so she visited Estes Park in 1873. Her experiences led to one of the first books to emphasize the area's wonders, *A Lady's Life in the Rocky Mountains.* The book was full of human interest, and descriptions like "The wild life was abundant, the trees uncut, and the wild flowers at their best." The popularity of *A Lady's Life* was instrumental in bringing tourism to Estes Park.

James Nugent
Isabella Bird declared Rocky Mountain Jim, "A man any woman might love but no sane woman would marry." He was described as an affable desperado with one eye, the other lost in a fight with a bear, and an affinity for violence and poetry. Nugent resisted the Earl of Dunraven's moves to acquire control of Estes Park, and was killed in a dispute over the issue.

Joel Estes
Exploration brought Joel Estes to the mountains to discover a beautiful valley where he would move his family. They were the first settlers, building

a cabin on Willow Creek in 1860. Long, cold winters with deep snow convinced Estes to sell the homestead for a team of oxen in 1866, and they returned to St. Joseph, Missouri.

William N. Byers, editor of the *Rocky Mountain News*, stayed with the family on his attempt to climb Longs Peak. His news article referred to the area around their homestead as "Estes' Park."

Abner Sprague

The Earl of Dunraven's expansions in Moraine Park were challenged in 1875 when Abner Sprague and others claimed land adjacent to the Earls'. By the 1890s, Abner and his wife, Alberta, understood that their ranch had promise as a resort when vacationers stopped to visit and request services. Visitors were eager to pay for accommodations, and the Spragues complied. Abner sold his resort in 1904 and opened another in Glacier Basin, operating it until 1943. The National Park Service removed Abner's Moraine Park Resort in 1962.

Abner Sprague, NPS archives

William Henry Jackson, U.S. Geological Survey archives

William Henry Jackson

A renowned Civil War photographer, Jackson helped promote railroads in the 1870s by chronicling the western landscape on their behalf. His sweeping, large-format black-and-white and color images of the Grand Canyon, Yellowstone, and Colorado advanced tourism in the Rocky Mountains.

James Grafton Rogers

Many advocates are required to establish a national park, especially those who understand legislation. Denver attorney James Rogers filled that role. Rogers was a mountaineer and explorer of Colorado's wild areas. He explored its valleys and climbed more than 17 of its 14,000-foot peaks. He helped organize the Colorado Mountain Club and became its first president. Rogers drafted the legislation that established Rocky Mountain National Park.

James Grafton Rogers, NPS archives

John Holzwarth Sr.

A saloonkeeper in Denver, John Holzwarth Sr. was forced out of his profession in 1919 because of Prohibition. He moved to the Kawuneeche Valley to raise cattle. The opening of the Fall River Road to Estes Park provided the opportunity for him to have a guest ranch. His Never Summer Ranch operated until 1974, when it was purchased by The Nature Conservancy, then given to the National Park Service. It is now the Holzwarth Historic District.

Freelan Oscar Stanley

With his twin brother Francis, F. O. Stanley designed and manufactured in 1897 a steam-powered automobile called the Stanley Steamer. The car's success and a photographic process they sold to George Eastman of Kodak fame made them rich. Six years later, F. O. was diagnosed with tuberculosis and moved from Maine to Colorado for his health. Liking what he found, he built the Stanley Hotel, and became an ally of Enos Mills in the creation of Rocky Mountain National Park.

F. O. Stanley, NPS archives

Enos Mills

Enos Mills, Library of Congress, LC-USZ62-105647

You may never have heard of Enos Mills, but his vision brought you here. Growing up in southeastern Kansas, Enos was afflicted with chronic, debilitating illnesses. Moving to a better climate was his best option. His older sister offered him a room where she lived in Greeley, Colorado. At 14 years old and alone, Enos hitchhiked to Kansas City and got a job in a bakery to earn enough money to make the 600-mile train trip to Colorado.

Enos was united with other family members in the Estes Park area. At age 15, he was guided up Longs Peak for the first of more than 250 ascents he would eventually make. He liked the area and began building a homestead cabin. The long winters forced him to seek employment elsewhere. The Anaconda Mining Company in Butte, Montana, hired him over the winters of 1887 to 1901.

A mine fire in 1889 prevented Mills from working so he took the opportunity to travel to San Francisco. While strolling North Beach, he came upon a pile of kelp. Curious about the seaweed, he turned to a passerby with questions. This was a chance meeting with John Muir. They shared stories: Muir about the Sierra Nevada, Mills about Longs Peak. Muir encouraged Mills to pursue his interests in the natural world and share them with the public.

Mills returned to Colorado, built Longs Peak Inn, and began taking visitors on nature walks. He honed a discovery style of presentation that led to the development of one of the first interpretive training programs. His Trail School nature guides became the first guides licensed by the National Park Service.

Mills wrote books on nature guiding, and for several years traveled across the United States giving lectures about the importance of saving natural areas like Longs Peak for future generations. His efforts were rewarded when an Act of Congress created Rocky Mountain National Park in January 1915. The *Denver Post* labeled him "The Father of Rocky Mountain National Park."

Enos Mills died in September 1922. His legacy remains in his many books, the lands he helped preserve, and the Enos Mills Cabin Museum, south of Estes Park.

Esther Burnell

Burnell fell in love with the Estes Park area while vacationing in 1916 with her sister, Elizabeth. She stayed to homestead. A year later, Enos Mills employed Esther and Elizabeth as guides at his Longs Peak Inn. Esther was recognized as the first licensed nature guide for the National Park Service, starting the long tradition of naturalists/interpreters. She married Enos in 1918.

TWO LEGISLATIVE ACTS THAT SCULPTED THE WEST

1862 Homestead Act

The purpose of the Homestead Act was twofold: to encourage settlement in the West and to exploit western forests to provide wood for construction in the East. Most people chose to farm rather than log.

The homesteader had to be the head of a household or at least 21 years old. They needed to claim and live on 160 acres, build a home, make improvements, and farm. Immigrants, single women, and former slaves who were citizens or declared their intent to become a citizen could apply. After five consecutive years of occupation, homesteaders "proved up" and were given title to the land.

MacGregor Ranch, 1893, NPS archives

1872 General Mining Act

The purpose of the act is to promote the development of mining resources. The General Mining Act states that anyone has the right to explore for and extract minerals from a tract of land in the public domain. Staking a claim means marking the boundaries, often with wooden posts. Then, the claim must be registered with the government at $5 per acre. With few changes, this act is still in effect.

ROCKY'S ARTIST-IN-RESIDENCE PROGRAM

William Allen White cabin, NPS photo, Katy Sykes

Artists evoke emotions and capture the spirit of people, places, and events through their unique ways of interpreting the world. Well before any national park existed, artists were influencing people to take action to protect America's special places. The Hudson River School of landscape artists had profound effects, shaping the way people saw themselves in nature. Nineteenth century photographers began using their media to capture events, drawing viewers into recorded moments. Painters like Thomas Moran and Albert Bierstadt and photographers such as William Henry Jackson and Ansel Adams interpreted the wonders in landscapes to inspire decision makers to save lands for future generations.

Today, painters, photographers, writers, sculptors, and performing artists including musicians and dancers express their visions of the meanings of landscapes through the National Park Service's Artist-in-Residence program. Artists live and work in the parks during two-week residencies, sharing their expressions and talents with visitors.

Rocky Mountain National Park's Artist-in-Residence program runs between June and September. It is housed in the historic William Allen White cabin in Moraine Park, built in 1887. White, a Pulitzer Prize winning writer, was a nationally recognized journalist, newspaper editor, and a strong advocate for Rocky. Refer to the park newspaper for the schedule of Artist-in-Residence presentations. Or visit White's cabin and meet the current artist.

BEST VISITOR CENTERS

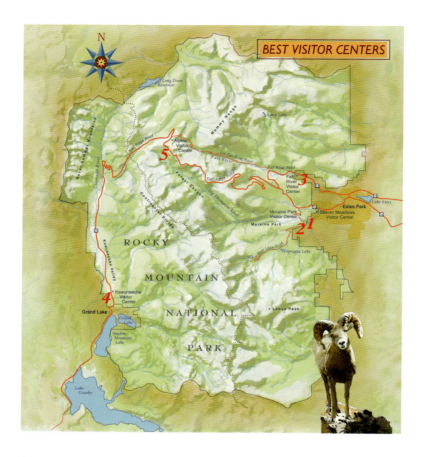

How will you know the best ways to use your time visiting Rocky? This book is intended to answer most of your questions, but speaking with a knowledgeable National Park Service employee or volunteer will greatly enhance your holiday. Get oriented; visit the five visitor centers located strategically throughout the park. Staff will provide current roadway and trail information, point you in the direction of facilities, and share how to best experience the park. Each visitor center has a unique theme. See all of them while on your discovery quest of Rocky Mountain National Park.

1. Beaver Meadows Visitor Center

The Beaver Meadows park entrance on Highway 36 is the highest volume entrance to Rocky. The visitor center has administrative offices, a theater featuring videos about park resources, an information desk, and a bookstore.

Beaver Meadows Visitor Center, NPS photo, Peter Biddle

2. Moraine Park Visitor Center

Do you have questions about the flora and fauna of the montane forests? This is a good place to have your questions answered. Whether you talk with a volunteer or park ranger, walk the self-guided nature trail, or view the wildlife exhibits, the Moraine Park Visitor Center is a good place to tour. Wondering about the local geology? The center has fine displays on the types of rock that form the mountains. The visitor center is on Bear Lake Road, 1.25 miles south from the intersection with Highway 36.

Moraine Park Visitor Center, NPS photo, Katy Sykes

3. Fall River Visitor Center

The first object that captures your attention upon entering the center is a life-size bronze statue of a running elk. The interpretive theme of the center is Rocky

Fall River Visitor Center, NPS photo, Katy Sykes

Mountain National Park through the seasons. Below the first floor is a discovery room, where children and adults are invited to touch objects and artifacts. Look for the Fall River Visitor Center along Highway 34 west of Estes Park, just before entering the national park.

4. Kawuneeche Visitor Center

South of the Grand Lake Entrance Station on Highway 34 is the Kawuneeche Visitor Center. Stop here to plan your visit and get up-to-date weather forecasts and Trail Ridge Road information. Displays here give an overview of the park's history, geology, and wildlife.

Kawuneeche Visitor Center, NPS photo, Peter Biddle

5. Alpine Visitor Center

Do you want to learn about the alpine tundra without hiking into it? The Alpine Visitor Center features displays about how life is adapted to this exceptional environment. Extraordinarily large viewing windows extend

Alpine Visitor Center, NPS photo, Peter Biddle

the length of the back wall, giving you sweeping views of the majestic tundra landscape. This is the premier visitor center in the park. It also has an information desk, a bookstore, a gift shop, and a café. The Alpine Visitor Center is at "the top of the world," 1 mile north of the Gore Range Scenic Overlook along Trail Ridge Road.

ROCKY'S SHUTTLE: LEAVE THE DRIVING TO US

All aboard, Alan Leftridge

Do you want to tour Trail Ridge Road yet have the freedom to investigate along the way? The park's free shuttle bus service allows you to enjoy the scenery without the distraction and bother of traffic and limited parking. It is the best way to relax and tour the park and share your experiences with fellow visitors. There are three shuttle bus routes: Moraine Park, Bear Lake, and Hiker Shuttle. The shuttles allow you to access many scenic destinations and trailheads. Planning ahead will help you get the most out of the shuttle system. Refer to the *RMNP Park News* (available at entrance stations and visitor centers) for up-to-date information about times and stops.

BEST SCENIC DRIVES

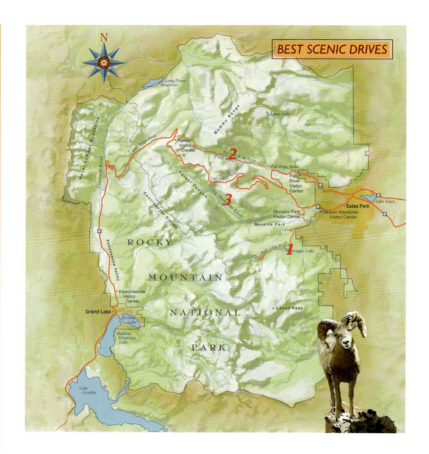

1. Bear Lake Road

Bear Lake Road leads you to several backcountry trailheads. Along the way, you will find a discovery center and nature trails that open windows of appreciation for the park's fauna, flora, and physical environment.

Bear Lake corridor, NPS photo, Ann Schonlau

Look for Bear Lake Road 0.25 mile inside the Beaver Meadows Entrance. The winding road ends in 9 miles at the Bear Lake parking area.

The Bear Lake area is one of the most popular spots in the park. The lake attracts many visitors because of its scenic beauty and easy access. Other visitors come here for the major trailheads to places like Dream Lake, Alberta Falls, Loch Vale, and Jewel Lake. Parking is difficult to find during the summer. Use the free shuttle bus system offered by the National Park Service to get to the Bear Lake area and the sites along the road.

Bear Lake Road, NPS photo, Ann Schonlau

Exclosures

Look for chain-link fences on either side of the road when you cross Beaver Brook. Exclosures are intended to keep out elk and mule deer. Look for others in montane areas like Horseshoe Park. Researchers examine how the area remains in a natural state, by excluding browsing animals. Notice that the fences do not reach the ground. Smaller animals like rabbits, bobcats, and coyotes gain easy access. You too can enter and explore the protected grounds through access gates. Compare what you see inside to the immediate area outside. Be sure to close the gate when you leave.

Moraine Park Discovery Center

The Discovery Center is 1.25 miles from the road's intersection with Highway 36. The building was once the Moraine Park Lodge, which included several cabins. Today, it houses interpretive exhibits about the wildlife and geologic history of Moraine Park. A self-guided nature trail focuses on montane flora.

Moraine Park Discovery Center, NPS photo

Moraine Park

West of the Discovery Center, across the road, is Moraine Park. The long low hill to the south is the south lateral moraine of a long-ago glacier that occupied today's meadow. The glacier left a depression filled with water from the Big Thompson River. Centuries of deposition from the river have filled the depression with rubble and silt.

Moraine Park, NPS photo, Jacob W Frank

Sprague Lake

Continue another 4.75 miles to the Sprague Lake turnoff. Early settler Abner Sprague built a lodge here and created the lake for his guests' angling pleasures. The lake remains but the lodge is gone. Today's visitor services include interpretive signage, a riding stable operation, and picnicking. Walk the 0.5-mile trail around the lake. The north and east shorelines provide beautiful views of the mountains—all over 12,000 feet—making up the Continental Divide. A calm day will give a glassy reflection off the water.

Bear Lake Road continues southwest for another 3.0 miles through young stands of aspen trees and lodgepole pines. Three switchback turns then take you over Bierstadt Moraine and to within 0.25 mile of your destination.

Sprague Lake, NPS photo

Bear Lake

The road ends at a large parking lot 9 miles from its junction with Highway 36. Rangers in an information booth at the head of the parking lot will help you plan your time here. First, however, take the self-guided nature trail around the lake.

Bear Lake, NPS photo

It offers a greater variety of attractions than most of the nature trails, plus it has some iconic views across the lake of the park's most famous peaks. Several benches line the trail. Plan time to pause and reflect on the serenity of the grand landscape.

2. Fall River Road

This road provides the best exploration you can have in Rocky Mountain National Park without getting out of your car to hike. The road passes through the montane and subalpine life zones to the alpine tundra. Drive the one-way 9.4-mile Fall River Road to its junction with Trail Ridge Road near the Alpine Visitor Center. Complete a loop by returning to Horseshoe Park via Trail Ridge Road.

Your adventure begins at the junction of Fall River Road with U.S. Highway 34, 2.2 miles inside the park from the Fall River Entrance west of Estes Park. Turn right on to Fall River Road toward Endovalley. The

Fall River Road and Mummy Range, NPS photo, Ann Schonlau

first 2 miles are paved and two-way. The Endovalley Picnic Area marks the beginning of the one-way gravel road. Drive the next 9 miles slowly—the posted speed limit is 15 miles per hour. Allow plenty of time to stop, but leave room for others to pass. Vehicles over 25 feet in length are prohibited.

Pick up a copy of the *Guide to Old Fall River Road* at any of the park visitor centers. The booklet provides a mile-by-mile description of what you will see, where to stop, and the natural and cultural heritage of the area.

You will be driving on part of the first road to cross the Continental Divide in this part of the Southern Rockies. Construction began in 1913 and took 7 years to complete. In those days, vehicles traveled in both directions. The road is narrow and steep, with switchbacks and no guardrails. Imagine navigating the road today if two-way traffic were still allowed!

Near the turnoff from the main road is a picnic area and the Lawn Lake Trailhead. The trail leads to Ypsilon Lake, Lawn Lake, and deeper into the high country.

Alluvial Fan

Less than 0.3 mile from Lawn Lake Trailhead, you will arrive at the Alluvial Fan area. Decades from now your grandchildren will still see the scars of the 2013 floods. Cloudbursts sent torrents of runoff that washed out this section of the road and scoured the thin soil away, leaving runoff rubble and little substrate for new vegetation to grow. The road was closed for more than a year to complete the repairs.

Just under 2 miles from here, the road divides, with the left fork leading to Endovalley Picnic Area. Go right to follow Fall River Road. This begins your climb to Fall River Pass, Alpine Visitor Center, and Trail Ridge Road.

Alluvial Fan, NPS photo, John Marino

Chasm Falls

Chasm Falls is 1.4 miles from the junction with Highway 36. Look for dippers near this 25-foot waterfall. The robin-size gray birds nest along the rushing creek, and can be seen hunting for insects in the turbulent waters.

Chasm Falls, NPS photo, Ann Schonlau

Willow Park

Continue another 1.5 miles to Willow Park. About 6,500 years ago, a glacier extended down the canyon. The ice left a terminal moraine and a depression that became filled with grasses and willows in this park. This is a good informal picnic spot.

Cañoncito

About 5 miles from the junction with Highway 36, pause to watch the waters of the Fall River cutting this little canyon. You are looking at about 7,500 years of erosion.

At about 11,000 feet above sea level, the road climbs out of the beautiful valley, above the treeline, and across the tundra for several miles to the Alpine

Visitor Center at Fall River Pass, where it joins Trail Ridge Road.

Fall River Pass

Many visitors assume that Fall River Pass is the Continental Divide. Instead, the divide is 4 miles west, along Trail Ridge Road at Milner Pass. Fall River Pass divides the Fall River drainage and the Cache la Poudre drainage.

Fall River Road, NPS photo, John Marino

You have reached Trail Ridge Road, and a decision: proceed west toward Grand Lake and explore the park west of the Continental Divide, or turn east, back toward Estes Park. A turn to the east will complete a loop.

3. Trail Ridge Road

Trail Ridge Road offers you the opportunity to discover the wonders of Rocky Mountain National Park's geology, and to learn about how the plants and animals who live here are adapted to this unique environment.

Most travelers on Trail Ridge Road enter Rocky Mountain National Park from the east. This description follows the east to west route.

You can get to Trail Ridge Road from either the Beaver Meadows Entrance on Highway 36, or the Fall River Entrance on Highway 34. The routes converge at Deer Ridge Junction, the beginning of Trail Ridge Road.

You can drive the next 40 miles in a little over an hour. Please don't. Plan to take more time than that to linger. Take in the wonders of the myriad sights. Get out of your car and listen to the wind, the call of birds, the bugle of elk, and the squeak of pikas. Smell the fragrant air. Feel the penetrating alpine sunshine. The road has too many stories to be appreciated in an hour. So, stop at the pullouts and visitor centers. Walk the nature trails. When you reach the end of the road, turn around. You will discover new wonders along your return.

Trail Ridge Road, NPS photo, John Marino

Deer Ridge Junction

This is the beginning of one of the nation's most famous roads, the highest continuous road in the country, taking you to the tundra and back. The road climbs 2,200 feet and every 1,000 feet gained in altitude is similar to traveling 400 miles toward the Arctic.

Hidden Valley

The valley got its name because it is hidden from Horseshoe Park, into which its waters flow. You will arrive at the Hidden Valley turnoff 2.5 miles from Deer Ridge Junction. The access road ends at a large parking lot with picnic tables, a warming hut, and an interpretive nature trail. Notice the long, narrow, treeless swath to the southwest. This is the route of a chairlift that ran until the 1980s. All other evidence of the Hidden Valley Ski Area is removed. In winter, the low rise just beyond the parking lot is still a popular sledding hill.

Many Parks Curve

You come to this spectacular overlook 1.6 miles southeast of Hidden Valley. Parking is provided on the right, after you make a sweeping turn. The overlook is named for its panoramic views of several parks. Signage directs you to Horseshoe Park, Beaver Meadows, Moraine Park, Little Tuxedo Park, and parts of Estes Park, with Longs Peak prominent to the southwest.

Rainbow Curve

Four miles from Many Parks Curve brings you to Rainbow Curve. Horseshoe Park is 2,000 feet below from the overlook. Let your eyes follow the meanders of the Fall River as it courses through the glaciated valley. To your right behind a glacial moraine is Hidden Valley. True to its name, the valley remains tucked away from sight. Rainbow Curve Overlook is 10,829 feet above sea level. You are nearing treeline, where a combination of high winds, little water, extreme temperatures, poor soil, and intense solar radiation conspire to halt forest advances. Notice the stunted firs and flagged trees.

Rainbow Curve Overlook, NPS photo, Walt Kaesler

Limber pines are adapted to these conditions, but instead of tall stately specimens, they are gnarled and twisted—testaments to the tenacity of life.

Forest Canyon Overlook

You have been passing through the tundra for the last 3 miles. Here is your first opportunity to experience this frigid zone firsthand; it's time for a short walk. Put on your warm clothing, grab your camera, and don't hurry—oxygen is in short supply at 11,716 feet. Your five-minute, 0.1-mile walk to the overlook passes through a delicate ecosystem in which some plants are more than a century old. Watch your step, and leave the flowers for the pollinators. The overlook provides a panorama of a classic U-shaped glacial valley, carved thousands of years ago by a massive river of ice. Across the

Forest Canyon Overlook, NPS, John Marino

canyon, see bowl-like depressions called cirques that were sculpted by mountain glaciers.

Rock Cut

Cross the open spaces of tundra on the Trail Ridge Road for 2 miles and you will reach Rock Cut. This is the highest point along the

Rock Cut, NPS photo, Ann Schonlau

road with a vehicle turnout and maintained access to this stunning environment. Here, you will find the 0.5-mile Tundra Communities Trail, interpreting the wonders of how plant life flourishes at 12,110 feet above the sea.

Lava Cliffs

The drive for the next 2.0 miles follows the Tundra Curves. Most of the road is at about 12,000 feet. This treeless area is windswept, with shattered rock outcroppings known as fellfields. The rocks are broken into small pieces by the actions of freezing and thawing. The tilting of the rocks results from frost expanding underground and heaving the surface skyward.

Lava Cliffs are a reminder that many geological forces have created Rocky Mountain's landscape. Volcanoes are often formed when tectonic plates collide. Compacted volcanic ash, known as tuff, flowed from volcanoes in today's Never Summer Mountains vicinity about 28 million years ago. The flow stopped here, forming these cliffs.

Your next stop is in 2 miles. Before reaching the Alpine Visitor Center, the road will reach its highest point, 12,183 feet.

Alpine Visitor Center, Alan Leftridge

Alpine Visitor Center

The unique log design on the roof captures snow and holds the shingles in place. Wind speeds here can exceed 100 miles per hour during severe winter storms.

The visitor center houses a restaurant, gift shop, and interpretive displays about the alpine tundra's plants, animals, and climate. Large viewing windows in the visitor center and a viewing platform around back offer a great vista down a glacial cirque and into the Fall River drainage.

Medicine Bow Curve

Prepare to stop 0.4 mile west of the visitor center. A switchback turn marks Medicine Bow Curve. On a clear day, the Snowy Range of Wyoming's Medicine Bow Mountains are visible 44 miles away. The drainage below is the Cache la Poudre River. It received its name from French fur trappers who cached supplies (including gunpowder) along its banks. They were pleased to return the next spring to find the cache undisturbed.

Trail Ridge Road loses nearly 1,000 feet over the next 4 miles to Milner Pass. You leave the tundra and encounter scattered Engelmann spruce trees. The trees become more protected from the cold drying winds as elevation decreases. Soon, the mixed forest is so dense that the trees grow right up to the pavement.

Milner Pass

The pass is named for T. J. Milner, an 1880s railroad promoter who surveyed a route through this vicinity. It is here that Trail Ridge Road crosses the Continental Divide. Precipitation falling west of the divide enters drainages that empty into the Pacific Ocean. The Atlantic Ocean is fed by moisture landing east of the divide.

Farview Curve

The lazy watercourse below you that meanders and spreads into marshes becomes the raging Colorado River in Arizona. Farview Curve looms more than 1,000 feet above the river and the Kawuneeche Valley (pronounced *kah-wuh-NEE-chee*, Arapaho for coyote). The turnout gives you a commanding view of the valley and the Never Summer Mountains dominating the western skyline.

Holzwarth Historic Site

Soon after leaving Farview Curve, the road rounds 5 tight switchbacks (each numbered on a road sign). The road then straightens the last 2.5 miles to Holzwarth Historic Site, once a family homestead and then dude ranch, with some 1920s-era buildings.

Holzwarth Ranch, NPS photo, William S. Keller

Kawuneeche Visitor Center

The Kawuneeche Visitor Center is at the western entrance of Rocky Mountain National Park, 7.8 miles from the Holzwarth Historic Site. Tour the center for the interpretive displays and share your experiences with fellow visitors.

If you are traveling from the west, this should be your first stop. The interactive displays and staff members will help you become acquainted with the park by informing you of guided walks, campfire programs, and visitor services.

Kawuneeche Visitor Center, NPS photo, Peter Biddle

BEST PICNIC AREAS

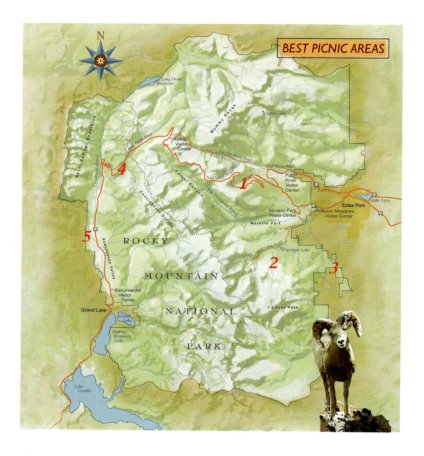

There are 18 established picnic areas in Rocky Mountain National Park, 10 on the east side and 8 on the west slope. Here is a list of the most desirable picnic areas.

Picnic Areas East Slope

1. Hidden Valley

The turnoff to this picnic area is 6.7 miles west of Beaver Meadows Visitor Center, along Trail Ridge Road. It is located at the site of former Hidden Valley Ski Area. The chairlift and lodge remnants were removed in the 1980s. Some of the wood used in the warming hut came from the lodge. The chairlift line remains as a swath through the trees. The beginner hill is at the head of the parking lot. Here you will find picnic tables sprinkled throughout the meadow. Hidden Valley Creek tumbles through the area, lined on both sides by a looped interpretive trail. Hike up the trail and find one of the secluded tables for your meal.

Hidden Valley, Alan Leftridge

2. Sprague Lake

Sprague Lake Picnic Area is 5.7 miles south of the junction of Highway 36 and Bear Lake Road. This is a lovely wooded spot adjacent to manmade Sprague Lake. Wildlife abounds in the area. Look for ducks, Clark's nutcrackers, gray jays, chipmunks, and golden-mantled ground squirrels. There are plenty of places to explore around the lake and creek. The views from the north end of the lake looking south are often stunning.

Sprague Lake, NPS photo, Walt Kaesler

3. Lily Lake

You will find this lake off Highway 7, about 7 miles south of Estes Park. Most visitors believe that they are no longer in Rocky Mountain National Park after leaving Estes Park. To their surprise, they learn

Lily Lake, Alan Leftridge

that this tranquil area is in the park. Therefore, pets are not allowed on the Lily Lake Trail. The setting is dramatic. Let the children play along the lakeshore, then after your meal take a walk around the lake.

Picnic Areas West Slope

4. Lake Irene

The picnic site is off Highway 34, about 16.5 miles north of Kawuneeche Visitor Center. The Lake Irene Picnic Area is on the west side of Trail Ridge Road, near Milner Pass, west of the Continental

Lake Irene Picnic Area, NPS photo

Divide. After your meal, explore Lake Irene by following the 0.5-mile loop trail around the lake. The trail is steep, but worth the effort for exploring the lovely area. Feeling more ambitious? Continue on the trail as it follows Phantom Creek southwest another 0.4 mile to a scenic viewpoint. The Never Summer Mountains and the Continental Divide command your attention to the west.

5. Coyote Valley

The picnic area is on Highway 34, about 7.5 miles north of Kawuneeche Visitor Center. Turn west, and drive on a dirt road 0.1 mile to the parking lot. Locate the trailhead and walk over the Colorado River bridge—you will see the picnic area to the

Coyote Valley Picnic Area, NPS photo, Russell Smith

southwest. The Coyote Valley Trail starts here. The picnic area is an excellent place to have your meal, before or after you have explored the trail.

PICNIC GUESTS

Don't be surprised if your picnic is suddenly interrupted by a loud bird call resounding from a tree branch overhead. A gray jay, rightfully called a "camp robber," has come to share your meal. The bird's repeated squawking will call even more jays to the presumed party. The birds might  distract you with their antics, but don't forget to guard your food.

The assault on your peaceful meal comes from the ground, too. Chipmunks and golden-mantled ground squirrels know to snatch food and scramble off into the bushes. Your relaxing picnic could easily become a competition. Don't expect this to happen every time you stop to eat outside, but it happens often. These animals are not tame, but they are habituated to humans. Birds and squirrels that live near where people eat have learned that bits and pieces of food are often left behind.

Because the animals are affable and entertaining, some people will feed them. They are doing the animals no favor. Feeding wildlife leads to problems. The animals become dependent on handouts and see it as an easy source of food. They can then become a bother around picnic areas and campgrounds. Another problem is that animals carry diseases that can be contracted by humans. Finally, human food denies them the nutrition they need to survive. Keep your picnic area and campsite clean and remember, do not feed the animals.

BEST HORSEBACK RIDES

Ready to ride, NPS photo, John Marino

Few experiences provide the feeling of travel in Old West style as a horseback ride.

Several stable operators offer trail rides from both the east and west sides of Rocky Mountain National Park. You can choose from short rides for the young or tenderfoot among us, all-day family adventures, or custom rides. Most of the trips are in the Roosevelt National Forest and the Arapaho National Forest. A few outfitters venture into the park. There are two stables in Rocky where the rides are solely in the park: Glacier Creek Stables (at Sprague Lake) and Moraine Park Stables. Saddle up and discover Rocky the Old West way!

BEST NAMES OF NATURAL FEATURES

Want some light-hearted fun? Review the park map of place names. Look for the names of mountains, lakes, rivers, creeks, ridges, and waterfalls. The origins of some of the names are obvious, others obscure. Many names are descriptive while some are lyrical. Most are documented, but the stories of a few are lost to antiquity. Here is a short list of some of the best names of natural features in the park.

Ypsilon Mountain, NPS photo, Jim Westfall

- **Rainbow Curve**
  When atmospheric conditions are right, this area is known for seeing single and double rainbows.

- **Never Summer Mountains**
  The Arapaho call them *Ni-chebe-chii*, meaning Never-No-Summer. The Colorado Geographic Board thought the name was difficult to say and preferred instead Never Summer Mountains.

- **Ypsilon Mountain**
  Snow stays long into the summer months in the clefts on the mountain, resembling the letter Y, the Greek alphabet symbol for Ypsilon.

- **Bierstadt Lake and Moraine**
  Both of these features were named for Albert Bierstadt, the famous Hudson River School painter of the 1800s. Bierstadt was brought to the region by the Earl of Dunraven to help the Earl select the most picturesque spot for his hotel.

- **Calypso Cascades**
  The cascades were named by botanist William Cooper for the patches of calypso orchids (fairy slippers) that grow along the Cony Creek Trail.

- **Chickaree Lake**
  Chickaree is a colloquial name for the red squirrel, common to the pine forests of Rocky Mountain National Park.

- **Colorado River**
  El Rio Colorado translated to Ruddy River. It was named by Spanish-speaking adventurers who saw the river closer to its mouth where it carries a lot of red sediment.
- **Keyboard of the Winds**
  This ridge between Longs Peak and Pagoda Mountain earned its name for the eerie sounds generated by high winds howling between the crags.
- **Sky Pond**
  Robert Sterling Yard, Chief of Education for the National Park Service until 1919, named this lake after being guided there by Abner Sprague.
- **The Twin Owls**
  This rock formation on Lumpy Ridge looms over Devils Gulch Road on the north side of Estes Park.
- **Mummy Range**
  The Arapaho called these mountains the White Owls. Albert Bierstadt may have suggested Mummy, and it stuck.
- **Lake of Many Winds**
  So named because the winds swirl around the lake as they blast through Boulder-Grand Pass at the Continental Divide.
- **Squeak Creek**
  The creek is named for Robert (Squeaky Bob) Wheeler, who operated a hunting and fishing camp near the North Fork of the Colorado River that he called "Hotel de Hardscrabble." Wheeler was tagged with his nickname for his high-pitched voice.
- **Dragons Egg Rock**
  Jack Moomaw named this feature on the south slope of Mount Meeker. He must have found just the right angle from which it looks like an egg. No one knows why the long-time Rocky Mountain National Park ranger gave it that name.

Play a game with your fellow travelers. See an interesting unnamed feature? Give it a name.

A CONCISE HISTORY OF ROCKY'S GEOLOGY

Three epic processes formed the landscape of Rocky Mountain National Park: rock formation, continental drift and uplift, and mountain carving.

Rock Formation

Longs Peak. NPS photo by David Pinigis

The rocks around you were formed long before the mountains. Hundreds of millions of years ago a shallow sea lay across this area. Water runoff from surrounding hills deposited mud. Dying shell life left behind lime. Layers of mud and lime collected, and their weight compressed earlier strata deep toward the earth's mantle. Pressure from above and heat from the mantle changed the deposits into sedimentary and metamorphic rocks, some estimated to be 1.8 billion years old.

Continental Drift and Uplift

From 50 to 70 million years ago, the driving thrust of continental drift forced the smaller Farallon tectonic plate from the west against the larger North American plate. The Farallon slid beneath the North American plate, pushing the Earth's crust upward. The period is named the Laramide orogeny. The relentless collision of the plates piled layers of crust on top of each other, building a broad backbone of mountains from Canada to Mexico.

Mountain Carving

The Laramide orogeny formed a high plateau, up to 20,000 feet above sea level, much like today's Tibet. Over the last 60 million years, glaciers, weathering, and water sculpted that high plateau into the dramatic peaks and exquisite valleys we see today.

Although the land that would become Rocky Mountain National Park remained covered in ice until about 11,000 years ago, the processes that built this landscape continue today. Several small glaciers continue to grind the ancient rocks in high mountain cirques. Water carries sediment down from the mountains into the Colorado River and Mississippi River watersheds.

41

TUNDRA ROCK ART: THE LICHENS

Lichen, Alan Leftridge

Those colorful patches affixed to the alpine tundra rocks are lichens. What you see could be any of about 1,500 species of scaly plants that consist of a symbiotic association of algae and fungi, growing as one. Indomitable, lichens are pioneer species living in harmony with sparse environments. They display manifold colors, textures, and growth designs that may have been developing for centuries.

Lichens help make soil. Through both pressure and chemical action, they infiltrate and wedge apart pieces of rock. Some of their acidic products dissolve the rock's surface, freeing mineral grains. This action is immeasurably slow, but the resilience and endurance of lichens puts time on their side. Look for nature's rock art as you walk the alpine tundra trails.

BEST SELF-GUIDED TRAILS

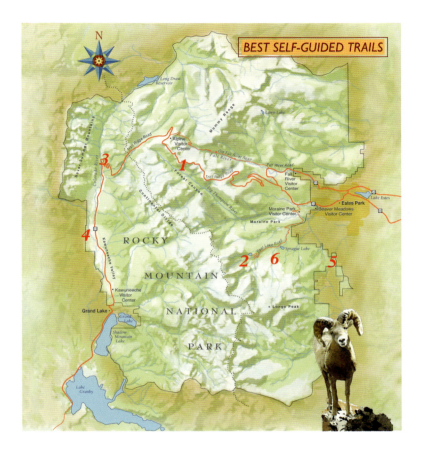

There are 355 miles of trails in Rocky Mountain National Park. Almost all of the trails are free of signage, allowing you to discover the wonders of the park on your own. The National Park Service has selected six trails, each representative of one of the park's themes, to interpret in a self-guided format. Visiting each trail will give you an overview of why Rocky was designated a national park.

1. Tundra Communities Trail

The Tundra Communities Trailhead is 12.9 miles west of Deer Ridge Junction, at Rock Cut, along Trail Ridge Road.

Visit the unique world of the alpine tundra. Here, there are only about 40 frost-free days per year, summer temperatures seldom reach 70°F, and snow can fall at any time. Interpretive signs introduce you to wildflowers that grow only in the Rocky Mountains. This is where some plants store energy for decades, before blooming just once, and then die. You will learn that a few animals, such as pikas, ptarmigans, and marmots, are adapted to live here year-round in extreme conditions that we cannot bear. You will also find a side trail that leads to rocks that millions of years ago were silt in a shallow seabed. The trail ends at 12,319 feet above sea level.

Tundra Communities Trail, NPS photo, Ann Schonlau

2. Bear Lake Nature Trail

Turn onto Bear Lake Road 0.25 mile inside the Beaver Meadows Entrance. The winding road ends in 9 miles at the Bear Lake parking lot and trailhead.

The Bear Lake Nature Trail is a 0.6-mile loop around the lake. The purpose of the trail is to introduce you to the natural history and cultural heritage of this subalpine region. Get the *Bear Lake Nature Trail* guidebook at the Bear Lake Ranger Station or the trailhead. This brochure anticipates many of your questions and will enhance your experience. Follow the key to the 30 spots along the trail that tell the story of the Bear Lake area.

Bear Lake Nature Trail, NPS photo, Peter Biddle

Bear Lake is a beautiful body of water, surrounded by a mixed forest. Several wooden benches are placed at picturesque spots along the trail. Relax and absorb the views, and ponder this captivating subalpine area.

3. Colorado River Trail (Lulu City)

The Colorado River Trail is 11.5 miles north of Grand Lake on the west side of Highway 34. Pick up a trail booklet at one of the visitor centers in the park before you take this trail.

Lulu City is a 6.2-mile round-trip hike from the trailhead. It is an easy-to-moderate hike, with an elevation gain of 300 feet. The trail leads you to an 1880s gold mining camp called Lulu City, and introduces you to the cultural heritage of the west slope. The camp featured a hotel, post office, courthouse, saloons, and lumber mills. Like so many other hopeful strikes in the Southern Rockies, the promise of riches was never realized—the ore was low quality.

Colorado River Trail, NPS photo, John Marino

A few foundations of wooden buildings remain. Explore the area and imagine what it must have been like to settle here with the hope of finding lifelong financial security.

4. Coyote Valley Trail

The Coyote Valley Trailhead is 7.5 miles north of Grand Lake off Highway 34, in the *Kawuneeche* Valley.

Kawuneeche is the Arapaho word for "coyote." The name fits, because this area is good habitat for wildlife including coyotes. Look also for moose, deer, songbirds, and many wildflowers. The National Park Service has placed

Coyote Valley Trail, NPS photo, Ann Schonlau

interpretive panels along the trail to help you appreciate this riparian habitat of the west slope. The trail is a 1-mile round-trip on a well-packed surface designed to accommodate wheelchairs. It follows the verdant banks of the Colorado River, with views of the Never Summer Mountains.

5. Lily Lake Trail

This trail is located 6 miles south of Estes Park along Highway 7.

Lily Lake is ideal for people who want to take a relaxed stroll in a beautiful setting. The short loop offers great views across the lake of Longs Peak, Mount Meeker, and Twin Sisters. Hiking up Lily Ridge to the north will enrich your experience at Lily Lake. You will find a commanding view of the montane lodgepole pine forest that encircles

Lily Lake Trail, NPS photo, Peter Biddle

the lake. The National Park Service provides an interpretive sign near the picnic area paying tribute to Enos Mills, who is regarded as the "Father of Rocky Mountain National Park." Although his homestead and lodge were not at Lily Lake, they were south on Highway 7 in a similar montane setting.

6. Sprague Lake Nature Trail

Look for Bear Lake Road 0.25 mile inside the Beaver Meadows Entrance. Turn right and follow the winding road about 6 miles to the Sprague Lake turnoff, then continue to the picnic area.

Sprague Lake Nature Trail, NPS archives

A footbridge leading from the parking lot crosses an inlet stream and connects with the nature trail. You will find a 0.8-mile loop around Sprague Lake with panoramic views of the Continental Divide. Before Rocky became a national park in 1915, the Sprague Lake area was the site of a mountain resort run by Abner and Alberta Sprague. The gravel trail features interpretive signage about the Sprague homestead and resort, and the trout lake that they developed for their visitors.

VISITING BEAR COUNTRY

Few sights evoke wildness more than a bear with cubs. The number of bears in the Rocky Mountain National Park region is unknown, but it is safe to say that they are common denizens. They are untamed and not interested in people. They prefer the valleys and the subalpine environments, but will roam. Think of yourself as a guest in their territory, and although you might not see a bear, they are near. To avoid a confrontation with a bear, follow these procedures and suggestions:

Black bear, NPS photo, Ann Schonlau

From Your Car

One of the most difficult things to do is drive past a bear. Your inclination is to stop and watch. Doing so can cause confusion for other motorists and be a hazard for the bear. If you must stop, do so at a safe distance at one of the turnouts. Use binoculars to view the bear and a telephoto lens to photograph the animal. Do not approach.

On a Trail

Bears use our trails. Avoid surprising a bear by being alert, hiking midday with a group, and making noise. Here are some suggestions that have worked for others who have happened upon a bear at close range:

- Never run! They are faster than you are. Back away.
- Speak to it in a low monotone, or not at all.
- Turn sideways, or bend at the knees to appear small.
- Avoid looking straight at the bear.
- Try to detour well around the bear so that your movements do not change its behaviors.

Do not approach, if you see a bear in a distant meadow or hillside. Stay the length of a football field away from any bear.

Read and follow the information on bears given to you at the park entrance. Look for updated information posted at trailheads.

The Best of Rocky

In Campgrounds

A bear's sense of smell is stronger than yours. Food odors attract them. When bears eat human food, unsafe conditions form that may lead to human harm and the bear being destroyed.

Bear-resistant trash cans, NPS archive

- All food and utensils must be stored in bear-proof containers.
- Keep coolers out of sight, even when empty. The open bed of a pickup truck is not sufficient.
- Do not burn food or trash in the fire pit.
- Place all trash in bear-resistant containers.

Camping in the Backcountry

Read the *Backcountry Camping Guide*, available online at www.nps.gov.

- Store food, cookware, toiletries, and garbage in a spare stuff sack and hang it at least 25 feet from the ground.
- Never cook, eat, or have food in your tent.
- Do not sleep in clothing that has food odors.
- Leave if a bear is frequenting the area.

Bear country, NPS archive

You assume risks being in bear country. Fortunately, confrontations are infrequent because bears avoid people, and visitors are committed to exercising good judgment.

HIKING IN ROCKY

Rocky Mountain National Park is a premier hiker's park, offering everything from easy strolls on paved surfaces to strenuous scrambles over broken rocks. The National Park Service maintains over 350 miles of trails here. Because the park is big and diverse, it can be difficult to select the best places to take a short walk. There are several trails that I consider the best for getting a flavor of the wild character of the park. Nature trails encourage you to learn about the natural and cultural heritage of Rocky at your own pace. Day hikes offer you half-day to full-day explorations of meadows, forests, and waterfalls. Here are 8 easy-to-moderate hikes covering some of the most iconic features of the park. The hikes take you to pristine lakes, memorable waterfalls, amazing vistas, and interesting historic sites. Get out of your vehicle to experience the sights, sounds, and fragrances of Rocky up close.

Hiking the Tonahutu Trail, NPS photo, Karen Daugherty

A Special Note

Annual visitation hovers around 3 million, with many people returning several times each year to hike to their favorite places. Many of the popular trailhead parking lots may be full before mid-morning. Use the park's free shuttle bus service, or arrive at your destination by early morning.

Be Prepared

Mountain weather is capricious. A sunny summer morning can become a cold, wet, and windy afternoon. Take warm, water-repellent clothing, hiking shoes, plenty of water, first-aid equipment, insect repellent, and maps. It is easy to become disoriented in the mountains. Stay on the trails!

Have ample provisions and clothing for hiking high-altitude trails. For added enjoyment, I recommend that you take snacks or a sack lunch on all of your hikes. Carry an extra bag to pack out your litter. Keep in mind that discarded orange peels, apple cores, sunflower seed shells, and pistachio nutshells take many years to deteriorate at these elevations, plus they are unsightly. Backcountry rangers have seen an increase in litter along trails and at picnic spots. Enjoy the backcountry, and help keep Rocky Mountain National Park as pristine as you found it.

BEST DAY HIKES

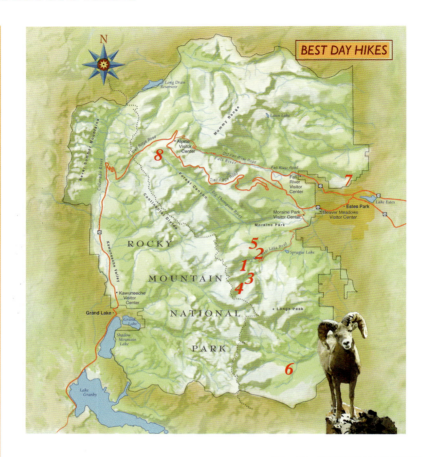

1. Bear, Nymph, Dream, and Emerald Lakes

Level of difficulty: Easy to moderate
Duration: 2 to 3 hours
Distance: 4 miles round-trip
Elevation change: 650 feet
Best time of the year: Anytime the trail is free of snow
Trailhead: From U.S. Highway 36, turn onto Bear Lake Road 0.25 mile inside the Beaver Meadows Entrance. Follow the winding road 9 miles to its end at the Bear Lake parking lot and trailhead.

Nymph Lake, Alan Leftridge

Notes: This is the most popular hiking area in Rocky due to its short trails, diverse beauty, and easy access to secluded valleys beneath soaring peaks. From the trailhead, follow the Bear Lake Trail 100 yards to Bear Lake. After walking around the lake, retrace your steps to the main trailhead and turn south toward Nymph Lake. You will arrive at Nymph Lake after hiking 0.5 mile on a well-packed trail. Flowering pond lilies cover much of the lake by midsummer. Walk another 0.6 mile to picturesque Dream Lake, staying right where the Glacier Gorge Trail splits left. Skirt the north side of Dream Lake and Tyndall Creek another 0.7 mile to Emerald Lake and trail's end. Boulders line the shore. Find a big rock, sit, and take in the splendor of the area.

Emerald Lake, NPS photo, Ann Schonlau

2. Bierstadt Lake

Level of difficulty: Easy
Duration: 2 hours
Distance: 3.2 miles round-trip
Elevation gain: 255 feet gain
Best time of the year: Anytime the trail is free of snow
Trailhead: From U.S. Highway 36, turn onto Bear Lake Road 0.25 mile west of the Beaver Meadows Entrance. Follow the winding road 9 miles to the Bear Lake parking lot and trailhead. (Several trails lead to Bierstadt Lake. The two most popular are from Bear Lake and the Bierstadt Lake Trailhead. The Bear Lake access is the easier, as described here.)

Notes: The lake is named for Albert Bierstadt, a 19th century artist who romanticized Longs Peak in his painting from near the

Bierstadt Lake, NPS photo, John Marino

junction of Fish Creek and Lake Estes. The picture once graced the U.S. Capitol rotunda.

From the trailhead, follow the Bear Lake Trail past Bear Lake and onto the Flattop Mountain Trail. Stay to the right and find the Bierstadt Lake Trail at 0.4 mile. The trail winds through aspen groves and pine forests most of the next mile. Bierstadt Lake is a marshy subalpine lake. A trail circles the lake providing views of Longs Peak and the Continental Divide, worthy of picture postcards.

3. Lake Haiyaha

Level of difficulty: Easy to moderate
Duration: 2+ hours
Distance: 4.2 miles round-trip
Elevation change: 745 feet
Best time of the year: Spring and autumn
Trailhead: From U.S. Highway 36, turn south at Bear Lake Road 0.25 mile inside the Beaver Meadows Entrance. The winding road ends 9 miles at the Bear Lake parking lot and trailhead.

Notes: Behind the Bear Lake information booth, find the trailhead to Emerald Lake. You will arrive at Nymph Lake after walking 0.5 mile. Stay on the Emerald Lake Trail as you walk around Nymph Lake.

Lake Haiyaha in winter, NPS photo, Chelsea Hernandez

After 0.6 mile, at the foot of Dream Lake, you will come to the junction with Lake Haiyaha Trail. Follow the trail to the left. Another 0.6 mile of walking through dense forest brings you to the trail that leads to Mills Lake and The Loch. Proceed straight. The last 50 yards before Lake Haiyaha is a jumble of boulders from the canyon ahead. The scene at Lake Haiyaha is impressive. High above the lake on your left is 12,486-foot Otis Peak. To your right is 12,713-foot Hallett Peak. The disorder of boulders at the head of the lake is Chaos Canyon. According to the U.S. Board on Geographic Names, *Haiyaha* is an American Indian word for "rock." Find a boulder to sit upon, and let the serene alpine environment envelop you.

4. The Loch

Level of difficulty: Moderate
Duration: 3+ hours
Distance: 6.1 miles round-trip
Elevation change: 730 feet
Best time of the year: Anytime the trail is free of snow
Trailhead: From U.S. Highway 36, turn onto Bear Lake Road 0.25 mile west of the Beaver Meadows Entrance. Continue 9.0 miles to the Bear Lake parking lot and trailhead.

The Loch, NPS photo, Chelsea Hernandez

Notes: Angle to your left as you approach the Bear Lake Trailhead. Cross over a bridge and continue left down the paved trail. Your first stop is at 0.9 mile, when you arrive at 25-foot Alberta Falls. It is considered one of the most spectacular water features in Rocky. You'll see why, as it rumbles down Glacier Creek. Beyond the falls, the trail rises, levels, then drops and passes through a centuries-old burn. The trail splits at 2.2 miles. Follow the directions posted on the sign. The Loch is one of the most popular backcountry destinations in the park. It is a favorite spot for photographers who seek images of the lake waters reflecting 13,153-foot Taylor Peak.

5. Cub Lake

Level of difficulty: Easy
Duration: 2 to 3 hours
Distance: 4.6 miles round-trip
Elevation change: 540 feet
Best time of the year: Anytime the trail is free of snow
Trailhead: From U.S. Highway 36, turn south onto Bear Lake Road 0.25 mile inside the Beaver Meadows Entrance. Continue 1.25 miles, then turn right toward Moraine Park Campground. Drive another 0.7 mile to the Cub Lake Trailhead on the left.

Notes: This is an easy hike through a forest and beside a stream, loved by children and casual walkers. The Cub Lake Trail is famous for passing through several plant and animal communities to a hidden lake. The trail crosses a bridge over the Big Thompson River, and then passes through thickets of willows as it skirts the western end of Moraine Park. At 0.5 mile the trail meets the South Lateral Moraine Trail; turn right here. You will encounter a series of beaver ponds as you parallel Cub Creek. The trail provides an easy walk through aspen groves, over slight rises, and into denser pine and spruce forests. Tall trees surround the water-lily-covered lake, but you will find plenty of seating areas on lakeside boulders. It is a great place for a family picnic.

Cub Lake, NPS photo, Chelsea Hernandez

6. Ouzel Lake

Level of difficulty: Moderate
Duration: 6 hours
Distance: 9.8 miles round-trip
Elevation change: 1,510 feet
Best time of the year: Anytime the trail is free of snow
Trailhead: The Wild Basin Trailhead is south of Estes Park, off Colorado Highway 7. Drive 12.5 miles south to Wild Basin Road. Turn west and drive 0.3 mile to the Wild Basin turnoff. Pass the park entrance station and drive 2.1 miles to the road's end in the parking lot.
Notes: This is a popular high-country hike that features three waterfalls. The

Hiker at Ouzel Falls, NPS photo, John Marino

trail passes Copeland Falls, Calypso Cascades, and Ouzel Falls before ending at 6.4-acre Ouzel Lake. Take the Thunder Lake Trail from the trailhead. Within 0.3 mile, you reach Copeland Falls. There are upper and lower falls, and both are worth exploring. At 1.8 miles, you arrive at Calypso Cascades, named for the calypso orchids (also known as fairy slippers) that grow in the cool shade. Ouzel Falls is an additional 0.9 mile along the trail. About half a mile beyond Ouzel Falls, the trail divides. Follow the left fork toward Bluebird Lake. The trail climbs briefly, then

Best Day Hikes

rolls along an open ridge with mountain views for about 1.5 miles to a spur trail to Ouzel Lake on the left. Follow the spur trail down into the valley, then past Chickadee Pond to the foot of forest-rimmed Ouzel Lake with 12,176-foot Ouzel Peak and 13,176-foot Copeland Mountain in the background.

7. Gem Lake

Level of difficulty: Moderate
Duration: 3 hours
Distance: 3.6 miles round-trip
Elevation change: 2,100 feet

Gem Lake, NPS photo, Jacob W. Frank

Best time of the year: Spring and autumn
Trailhead: From U.S. Highway 34 in Estes Park, turn north on MacGregor Avenue. After a sharp right turn, MacGregor Avenue becomes Devils Gulch Road. Follow Devils Gulch Road 2 miles to the Lumpy Ridge Trailhead on the left.

Notes: This hike offers a great family outing in the early spring for glorious scenery and wildflowers. Gem Lake's close proximity to Estes Park makes it a popular early morning hike. Your venture will take you on a trail that climbs through mature ponderosa pine and aspen groves, and around granite boulders. Hike the trail in the springtime for the profusion of wildflowers, and in the autumn for the brilliant golden aspen leaves. About 0.5 mile from the trailhead, turn right at the junction with the Black Canyon Trail. After negotiating several switchbacks and stone stairs, you will arrive at Gem Lake. It is shallow, and sits in a rock amphitheater-like depression. The rock and treeline shore provide a magnificent scene. Be sure to bring snacks; it's a great place to linger and reflect on the tranquility of this unique backcountry area.

8. Ute Trail

Level of difficulty: Easy
Duration: 2 hours
Distance: 4.5 miles one way
Elevation change: 1,038 feet loss
Best time of the year: Summer
Trailhead: The trailhead is west of Trail Ridge Road at the Alpine

The Best of Rocky

Visitor Center, 21.5 miles from Beaver Meadows Visitor Center.

Notes: This section of the Ute Trail connects the Alpine Visitor Center to Milner Pass, at the Continental Divide. You will need to leave a car at Milner to shuttle you back to the visitor center, or retrace your steps.

The trail begins across Trail Ridge Road from the visitor center. This almost all-downhill walk begins in open alpine tundra. Trail Ridge Road is lost from sight after 0.5 mile, and you are enveloped in the solitude of the alpine tundra, where the only sounds are your footsteps and the breeze. To the north are the Cache la Poudre Valley and mammoth Specimen Mountain. Ahead of you are the snowy Never Summer Mountains. These will remain visible for half of your hike.

Ute Trail, NPS photo, John Marino

At around 2 miles, you reach a series of shallow ponds, then Forest Canyon Pass at 2.3 miles. This is the halfway point to Milner Pass.

You soon reach treeline and as you descend, you pass through patches of krummholz, then larger and more widely spaced subalpine fir and Engelmann spruce trees. The remainder of your hike is through denser forest groves, past a Precambrian rock formation known as the Poudre Lake Spires, and down to Poudre Lake on Milner Pass.

TRAIL ETIQUETTE

You may find total solitude on your hike, but chances are you will meet others. Consider the following while on the trail:

Take time to acknowledge other hikers. Say hello, and exchange information about trail conditions, wildlife, and scenery.

Parks are for people, but we can unintentionally destroy what we love. Lessen damage to Rocky. Stay on the trail; cutting switchbacks and making shortcuts causes erosion.

Always yield to uphill hikers. Show courtesy by stepping aside and allowing hikers traveling uphill to keep their pace.

Equestrians share many of the trails with hikers. When encountering a mounted horse, step off the trail to the downhill side.

Apple cores, banana skins, and orange peels are human food scraps. None are in natural wildlife diets. Refrain from leaving these and all food items behind, thinking that animals will appreciate the nourishment. The scraps are slow to decompose, are unsightly, and are unhealthy for wildlife.

Leave no trace that you visited.

BEST WATERFALLS

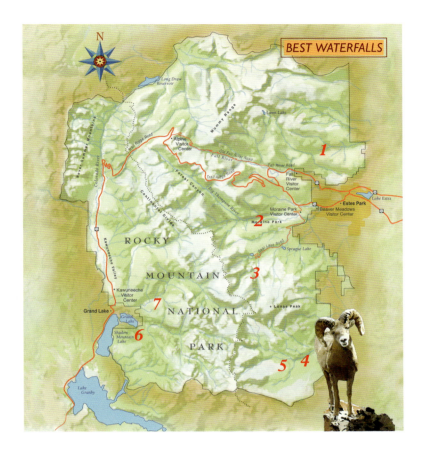

Rocky Mountain National Park has 473 miles of streams that tumble from the high country toward the plains below. Innumerable waterfalls are found throughout the park, some seasonal, others year-round. Most are in the backcountry, requiring moderate to strenuous hikes to locate. Here are some iconic waterfalls where casual visitors can walk. Waterfalls are favored spots for picnics. Remember to pack your lunch!

1. Bridal Veil Falls
MUMMY RANGE AREA
Waterfall drop: 55 feet
Level of difficulty: Moderate
Duration: 4 to 5 hours
Distance: 6.4 miles round-trip

Elevation change: 1,060 feet elevation gain

Trailhead: From Estes Park, drive 4 miles north on Devils Gulch Road to McGraw Ranch. Turn left on McGraw Ranch Road and drive 2 miles to the Cow Creek Trailhead.

Notes: Are you looking for solitude? This is an excellent morning hike in a secluded area of the park. Much of your walk will be through open forests and meadows. You will likely see a lot of wildlife along the margins. The trail slopes up into a canyon, and the last mile winds upward following Cow Creek through an aspen grove. You will encounter some rocky steps before reaching Bridal Veil Falls, nestled in a narrow canyon.

Bridal Veil Falls, NPS photo, Ben Hoppe

2. Fern Falls

MORAINE PARK AREA
Waterfall drop: 60 feet
Level of difficulty: Easy
Duration: 3 hours
Distance: 5.2 miles round-trip
Elevation change: 700 feet elevation gain

Trailhead: From Bear Lake Road, turn west on Moraine Park Road. Just before the Moraine Park Campground, turn south on Fern Lake Road and drive 2 miles to the Fern Lake Trailhead.

Notes: The Fern Lake Trail is listed on the National Register of Historic Places mostly because of its value to tourism in the early 1900s. You will understand why as you traverse forest floors covered in ferns, see the Big

Fern Falls, NPS photo, Jacob W. Frank

Thompson River with the surrounding mountains, and arrive at an area known as The Pool, where the Forest Inn once stood. As if all this weren't enough, you'll discover Fern Falls, a lovely plunge in Fern Creek.

3. Alberta Falls
BEAR LAKE AREA
Waterfall drop: 25 feet
Level of difficulty: Easy
Duration: 1 hour
Distance: 1.7 miles round-trip
Elevation change: 160 feet elevation gain
Trailhead: Drive about 8 miles up Bear Lake Road and park at the Glacier Gorge Trailhead.
Notes: Alberta Falls is one of the most popular hiking destinations in the park. You will see why, as you discover the water hurling through a deep ravine on Glacier Creek.

Alberta Falls, NPS photo, Chelsea Hernandez

Abner Sprague named the waterfall for his wife Alberta. The Spragues were early residents in what is now Rocky Mountain National Park.

4. Copeland Falls
WILD BASIN AREA
Waterfall drop: 30 feet
Level of difficulty: Easy
Duration: 1 hour
Distance: 0.9 mile round-trip
Elevation change: 75 feet elevation gain
Trailhead: From Estes Park, drive 12.5 miles south on Colorado Highway 7. Turn right onto Wild Basin Road. Proceed another 2.4 miles on a narrow gravel road to the trailhead. Wild Basin is very popular. Arrive early to secure parking.
Notes: Walk through a beautiful and pristine subalpine forest to Lower Copeland Falls, just 0.3 mile from the trailhead. Follow the creek bank another 100 yards to the upper falls.

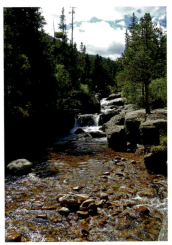
Copeland Falls, Alan Leftridge

5. Ouzel Falls

WILD BASIN AREA
Waterfall drop: 40 feet
Level of difficulty: Easy
Duration: 3 hours
Distance: 5.4 miles round-trip
Elevation change: 950 feet elevation gain

Trailhead: From Estes Park, drive 12.6 miles south on Colorado Highway 7. Turn right onto Wild Basin Road. Proceed another 2.5 miles on a narrow gravel road to the trailhead. Wild Basin is very popular. Arrive early to secure parking.

Notes: Casual travelers find the trail to Ouzel Falls an entertaining day hike. Most of the walk is along North St. Vrain Creek, affording you easy grades and plenty of stream access to explore the rich riparian zone. Along the way, you will pass Copeland Falls at 0.3 mile, and Calypso Cascades at 1.8 miles.

Ouzel Falls, NPS photo, Chelsea Hernandez

6. Adams Falls

GRAND LAKE AREA
Waterfall drop: 55 feet
Level of difficulty: Easy
Duration: 1 hour
Distance: 0.9 mile round-trip
Elevation change: 115 feet elevation gain

Trailhead: The East Inlet Trailhead is 2.4 miles from Grand Lake. From the junction of Highway 34 and CO 278, drive 0.3 mile east. Continue east on West Portal Road 2.1 miles to the parking area.

Notes: Its original name, Ousel Falls, tells you that dippers (water ouzels) frequent the area. It was renamed for Jay E. Adams, an early settler in the Grand

Adams Falls, NPS archive

Lake area. The trail's rockwork was built using native materials by the Civilian Conservation Corps and the National Park Service. Because of its history and construction methods, the East Inlet Trail is listed on the National Register of Historic Places.

7. Cascade Falls
GRAND LAKE AREA
Waterfall drop: 45 feet
Level of difficulty: Moderate
Duration: 3 to 4 hours
Distance: 6.8 miles round-trip
Elevation change: 430 feet elevation gain
Trailhead: From Highway 34 in Grand Lake, turn onto CO 278 (West Portal Road) and drive 1 mile to Route 663. Turn left, go 0.2 mile, and turn right to reach the North Inlet Trailhead.

Notes: The North Inlet Trail is a section of the 3,100-mile Continental Divide National Scenic Trail, spanning the Rocky Mountains from Canada to Mexico. The trail skirts Summerland Park, where wildlife abounds, before reaching the base of Cascade Falls at 3.4 miles. The spectacular, multi-step cascade gushes through a narrow rock cleft.

Cascade Falls, NPS photo, John Marino

BEST FISH

Rocky Mountain National Park is the headwaters for the Colorado, Big Thompson, Cache la Poudre, and Fall Rivers. The upper reaches and tributaries of these rivers provide pristine high-country habitat for native and non-native fish. The two iconic native fish in Rocky Mountain National Park are the greenback cutthroat trout and the Colorado River cutthroat trout.

Greenback Cutthroat Trout
Oncorhynchus clarki stomias

Agricultural water diversion, mining sediment runoff, and overfishing almost destroyed all populations of the greenback cutthroat.

Greenback cutthroat trout, USFWS photo

Then a pure strain was discovered in 1973. Brought back from extinction, it now occupies less than 1 percent of its historical range. The greenback cutthroat trout was selected in 1984 as the Colorado state fish.

Colorado River Cutthroat Trout
Salmo clarki pleuriticus

Colorado River cutthroat trout inhabit sections of the Colorado River drainage. The introduction of brook trout along with other non-native species has reduced their numbers.

Colorado River cutthroat trout, NPS photo, Debbie Biddle

NON-NATIVE FISH THREATEN NATIVE FISH POPULATIONS BY:
- *Preying on them.*
- *Outcompeting for food.*
- *Bringing diseases that the native fish cannot resist.*
- *Interbreeding with native fish.*
- *Outnumbering them in lakes, rivers, or streams.*

Three non-native fish are often associated with the Rocky Mountains: brown trout, rainbow trout, and brook trout.

Brown Trout
Salmo trutta

Stocks of brown trout were brought from Germany and Scotland in the 1880s. They were introduced into 38 states by 1900. The fish flourished in their new habitats.

Brown trout, NPS photo

Rainbow Trout
Salmo gairdneri

The rainbow trout is native to the tributaries of the Pacific Ocean in North America and Asia. The fish were introduced to Colorado and became the main fish stocked in the state.

Rainbow trout, NPS photo

Brook Trout
Salvelinus fontinalis

"Brookies" are native to the northeastern United States and the Appalachian Mountains to Georgia. They were brought to Colorado in 1872 and found the waters

Brook trout, NPS photo

ideal, soon out breeding all other species of fish. The brook trout is the state fish of eight states, including Michigan, New Hampshire, New Jersey, New York, Pennsylvania, Vermont, Virginia, and West Virginia.

BEST FISHING

Rocky is an angler's paradise, known for good fly-fishing. Populations of rainbow, brown, brook, cutthroat, and greenback cutthroat trout inhabit park waters. Many anglers come to Rocky for the allure of the scenery and the excitement of landing a wild trout. Because many streams here are small and shallow, there are few trophy-size fish. Also, most easily accessed spots are fished heavily. For the best fishing, go off the beaten path. Follow a stream toward its headwaters or hike to a backcountry lake. Look for places that show little sign of foot traffic. You will not need to hike far.

At high elevations, the fishing season is short. Alpine lakes may not be free of ice until mid-July, while most streams are generally accessible from April into October.

Fishing in the park is regulated to balance recreational opportunities with efforts to restore and sustain the fisheries. A valid Colorado fishing license is required for anyone 16 years of age or older. On waters that are catch-and-release only, bait and barbed hooks are not allowed. A few lakes and streams are closed to fishing seasonally or year-round. Regulations change: check at a visitor center for up-to-date information before you fish. Also, to avoid spreading invasive aquatic organisms, follow park guidelines to disinfect your waders and other fishing gear.

Best Lake Fishing

Sandbeach Lake: greenback cutthroat trout (catch-and-release only)
The Loch: brook and greenback cutthroat trout
Lily Lake: greenback cutthroat trout (catch-and-release only; east shore is closed May-June)
Sprague Lake: brook, brown, and rainbow trout
Lake Verna: brook trout

Fish are biting at Sprague Lake, NPS photo, Debbie Biddle

Best Stream Fishing

Cow Creek: brook and brown trout
Big Thompson River: brook, brown, rainbow, and greenback cutthroat trout (North Fork above Lost Falls is catch-and-release only)
Cub Creek: brook and brown trout
Colorado River: brook and brown trout
Black Canyon Creek: brook trout

BEST BIRDS

Colorado is home to 495 bird species, and Rocky Mountain National Park's diverse habitats harbor more than 280 of them. The park is designated a Global Important Bird Area by the National Audubon Society. Several species are iconic representatives of the park. You will have many opportunities to observe some of these birds in their natural settings. Understanding their diversity and adaptation to this environment will increase your enjoyment.

Broad-tailed hummingbird
Selasphorus platycercus

If you were as small as a broad-tailed hummingbird, you would be concerned about cold mountain nights. The bird is evolved to react to low temperatures by entering a state of slowed metabolic rate called torpor. The process allows them to maintain a safe body temperature.

Broad-tailed hummingbird, NPS photo, Jacob W. Frank

Broad-tailed hummingbirds feed on flower nectar from columbines, paintbrush, sages, currants, and glacier lilies. They supplement their diet with small insects that they catch midair and those they find under leaves.

Unable to walk, they get around solely by flight, beating their wings at a frequency of 50 times per second.

Where You Might See Broad-tailed Hummingbirds

You will find broad-tailed hummingbirds in subalpine meadows and shrubby areas near forests of willow, pine, fir, or spruce.

Ruby-crowned Kinglet
Regulus calendula

Ruby-crowned kinglets seem hyperactive as they dart among the foliage, fluttering their wings. About the length of the width of your hand, their complex and loud songs belie their small size and can be heard from afar. Kinglets

Ruby-crowned kinglet, USFWS photo, Donna Dewhurst

forage in treetops or in brush, searching for spiders, aphids, wasps, ants, bark beetles, and other insects.

Where You Might See Ruby-crowned Kinglets

You will find kinglets in the springtime in tall, dense Douglas-fir forests. For the remainder of the summer season, look for kinglets in shrubby areas along roads and trails.

Pygmy Nuthatch
Sitta pygmaea

As light as two nickels in the palm of your hand, pygmy nuthatches will go to battle with squirrels and other large predators. They can peck out their own nesting cavity in a tree, but they usually enlarge an existing hole, which they fiercely defend by blocking the entrance with their bodies.

Pygmy nuthatch, NPS photo

Nuthatches are always in motion, searching for food. Favoring ponderosas and other pines, they use their long, solid beaks to probe beneath bark and in needle clusters for seeds and insects. Pygmies are highly social, roosting with their own kind. Look for them flocking among the pines with other nuthatches, chickadees, and kinglets.

Where You Might See Pygmy Nuthatches

Listen for pygmies' constant squeaks, piping, and twittering in pine and aspen forests throughout the park.

Black-capped Chickadee
Poecile atricapillus

Like a sentry, the black-capped chickadee sounds the predator alarm for others in the flock. The more *dee* notes in a *chick-a-dee-dee-dee* call, the higher the threat level. Researchers have found that pygmy owls provoke the most *dees*, as high as 17.

Black-capped chickadee, NPS photo, Walt Kaesler

Chickadees spend much of the day picking small insects such as caterpillars off trees. They do not migrate, but flock and travel in foraging groups.

When food is abundant, they hide seeds and other food, and can remember thousands of hiding places. Every autumn, some of their brain neurons containing old information die and are replaced with new neurons that help them adapt to changes in their social flocks and their environment.

Listen for their two-tone call as you walk through forest groves. Do they see you as a threat? Count the number of *dees* in their call.

Where You Might See Black-capped Chickadees

You will see chickadees throughout the park in stands of lodgepole pine and Douglas-fir.

Mountain Chickadee
Poecile gambeli

Mountain chickadee, NPS photo, Russell Smith

The mountain chickadee and black-capped chickadee are cousins. They get along well and often travel and feed together. Whereas the black-capped chickadee has its characteristic *chick-a-dee-dee-dee* call, the mountain chickadee call sounds like *cheese-bur-ger*.

Locate a mountain chickadee and you will see it is not alone. They travel in pairs or small groups during the summer, acrobatically clinging to small limbs or hanging upside down from pinecones as they feed on insects and seeds. Wintertime finds them flocking with black-capped chickadees, nuthatches, and brown creepers, following each other one by one from tree to tree, searching for seeds. Some ornithologists speculate that the multi-species flock is a way to protect the birds from predators. Each species has its specialized way of detecting danger and warning others. When you find a mountain chickadee, look for its traveling companions.

Where You Might see Mountain Chickadees

You will likely see mountain chickadees in Douglas-fir and lodgepole pine forests.

American Dipper
Cinclus mexicanus

American dipper, NPS photo, Russell Smith

If you want to see a dipper, search for bird droppings on the boulders in fast-moving creeks. This is a sign that North America's only aquatic songbird is present. Its name comes from its bobbing motion when standing. About the size of a young robin, with a short tail, dippers build nests on creek bank ledges, behind waterfalls, and on boulders in rushing water.

Their ability to walk and swim underwater to catch insects is fun to watch. They disappear into a creek, leaving you to guess where they will emerge. They do not migrate, but may relocate to neighboring lakes in the winter to take advantage of insect hatches.

The Old World name, water ouzel, is still used in some places. It comes from the Old English "osle," meaning "blackbird."

Where You Might See Dippers

Dippers are common along fast-moving streams in the lower montane, where water courses over and around boulders.

Western Tanager
Piranga ludoviciana

Western tanager, NPS photo, Jacob W. Frank

Their near parrot-like plumage gives western tanagers a striking contrast to their open forest habitat. Yet their reclusive life in the upper reaches of the forest canopy makes tanagers difficult to find. Tanagers spend most of the day searching branches and flowers for insects. You can catch sight of one when it darts flycatcher-style into the open to snatch an insect. You might hear a western tanager before you see one. Its song is melodious and robin-like.

Where You Might See Western Tanagers

Western tanagers are closely associated with open Douglas-fir forests, which tend to favor north-facing slopes.

Steller's Jay
Cyanocitta stelleri

Steller's Jay, NPS photo, Ann Schonlau

Like its eastern cousin the blue jay, the Steller's jay is noisy. The bird's intonations are often mistaken for the screams of eagles and hawks. The jay's range of vocalizations is remarkably broad, including scratchy sounds, mimics of other birds, chirping squirrels, meowing cats, wailing dogs, cooing chickens, and even mechanical objects. Steller's jays are sociable, traveling in groups. Watch them playing with or chasing each other within the forest canopy. Year-round residents, they stash pine seeds for winter food.

Where You Might See Steller's Jays
Steller's jays live throughout the park and are often found where there is a closed forest canopy.

Gray Jay
Perisoreus canadensis

These medium-size forest denizens glide silently among the conifers, and before you know it, a group has encircled your picnic table or campsite. Also known as "camp robbers," they can become a nuisance as they attempt to steal your food.

They are found year-round throughout Rocky Mountain National Park. Nesting begins in March, while snow is still on the ground, in temperatures as low as -20°F. Females protect the eggs with their thick plumage and a well-insulated nest. They are omnivores that hoard food by using their sticky saliva to glue food bits to tree branches above the height of the eventual snow line.

Gray jay, NPS photo, Ann Schonlau

Where You Might See Gray Jays
Look for gray jays in campgrounds and picnic areas.

Clark's Nutcracker
Nucifraga columbiana

Clark's nutcracker, NPS photo, Jacob W. Frank

The Clark's nutcracker hides thousands of seeds each year. Unlike your neighborhood squirrel, the bird has a good memory and can find most of the seeds, even nine months later. Those seeds that they miss often germinate, thereby advancing the forest.

Stashing food allows this year-round resident to begin nesting in late winter. Both the male and female incubate the eggs. Each takes its turn while the other departs to feed at one of their seed caches.

Where You Might See Clark's Nutcrackers
Nutcrackers nest in conifers near treeline. Watch for them (and listen for their raspy calls) from trails and roads as you near the alpine zone.

Black-billed Magpie
Pica hudsonia

Black-billed magpie, NPS photo, Ann Schonlau

Many visitors from outside the Rocky Mountains are startled the first time this colorful long-tailed bird zips before their windshield. The bird might be racing to capture a small animal or insect. Their diet is broad and includes fruits, seeds, and carrion. These flashy relatives of jays and crows create a constant stream of raucous calls when they gather over a meal.

Black-billed magpies associate with people. Meriwether Lewis declared that magpies raided their tents for food. Keep your food properly stored, or you might be inviting an unintentional guest for a meal.

Where You Might See Black-billed Magpies
Residents of the open montane forests and meadows, magpies are easy to identify even at a distance thanks to their long tails and striking black and white markings.

Northern Flicker
Colaptes auratus

You are walking through a forest that has dense undergrowth. Without warning, you hear a thunder of flapping wings a few feet in front of you. Startled, you stop short. You have just experienced a northern flicker escaping your presence.

Northern flicker, NPS photo, Ann Schonlau

Although northern flickers can climb trees and hammer like other woodpeckers, they prefer not to. Ants make up their main diet, so they dig in the dirt and tear apart rotten logs to find them. Then, they use their long, barbed tongue to lap up the ants.

Northern flickers excavate holes in dead or diseased tree trunks for nesting. Quaking aspens, which are prone to heart rot, are a favored tree.

Where You Might See Northern Flickers

You can find northern flickers in montane and subalpine forests up to the treeline. They prefer areas with rotting logs.

Red-naped Sapsucker
Sphyrapicus nuchalis

Contrary to their name, red-naped sapsuckers do not suck sap. Instead, they have a specialized way of sipping it. Their tongue tips have small paintbrush-like projections that soak up the sap. The sap comes from shallow holes that the birds drill in the trunks of trees. They prefer aspen, willow, and mountain ash trees. Their diet is not restricted to sap; they also consume fruit and a wide variety of insects.

Red-naped sapsucker, NPS photo, Sally King

Where You Might See Red-naped Sapsuckers

Look for drill holes on the trunks of trees in the mixed montane forests that include willows and aspens. Then listen for the rat-a-tat-tat of a beak on wood and watch for a flash of red.

White-tailed Ptarmigan
Lagopus leucurus

White as snow in winter but displaying speckled mixed tundra colors in summer, the male white-tailed ptarmigan (pronounced, *TAR-muh-gan*) lives its life in the alpine regions of Rocky Mountain National Park. You may come across a ptarmigan on one of your hikes. If you do, expect to be startled. They are so well camouflaged that they will flee danger only at the last moment, bursting into flight as they escape.

Winter plumage, NPS photo, Karen Daugherty

Ptarmigan live a sedentary life in winter. They conserve energy by avoiding flight. When they venture from their roosting spot, they find it easy to walk on soft fluffy snow because of the extra feathers on the tops and bottoms of their feet. These extra feathers make their feet into snowshoes. The scientific name for the ptarmigan means "hare-footed mountaineer."

Where You Might See Ptarmigans

Warm weather can stress ptarmigans. They can be seen sheltering in snowbanks when temperatures exceed 70°F.

Summer plumage, NPS photo, Karen Daugherty

American Kestrel
Falco sparverius

The American kestrel is found in more places than any other bird that inhabits Rocky. From Alaska to the tip of South America, this small falcon lives in open country, farmland, forest edges, and even cities. Sometimes called a "sparrow hawk," its diet includes small rodents and insects.

American kestrel, NPS photo, Jim Peaco

Where You Might See American Kestrels
Look for kestrels perched atop dead trees and posts in the montane meadows of eastern Rocky. You might see one hovering against a breeze before it dives to capture its prey.

Golden Eagle
Aquila chrysaetos

Golden eagle, NPS photo, Watson

A golden eagle icon appears on more national emblems than any other animal, including the countries of Albania, Germany, Austria, Mexico, and Kazakhstan.

These eagles are mountain residents, living up to treeline. They often nest on cliffs in canyon and rimrock environments, but may also build in trees, on the ground, or in human-made structures.

While soaring at great heights, golden eagles exhibit astounding maneuverability. When locked in on their prey, they can dive at speeds close to 200 miles per hour. Hares, rabbits, ground squirrels, prairie dogs, and marmots have little chance of escaping this highly evolved predator.

Where You Might See Golden Eagles
Look up! You will most likely see this broad-winged predator soaring above the mountains, tundra, and meadows.

A SHORT CHECKLIST OF ROCKY'S BIRDS:	
_____ American Kestrel	_____ Golden Eagle
_____ Black-billed Magpie	_____ Gray Jay
_____ Black-capped Chickadee	_____ Northern Flicker
_____ Mountain Chickadee	_____ White-tailed Ptarmigan
_____ Broad-tailed Hummingbird	_____ Red-naped Sapsucker
_____ Pygmy Nuthatch	_____ Ruby-crowned Kinglet
_____ Clark's Nutcracker	_____ Steller's Jay
_____ American Dipper	_____ Western Tanager

BEST MAMMALS

The rugged Rocky Mountains with their severe climate and long winters have forced each mammal species to develop remarkable adaptations for survival. During the warm months, many of the animals are camouflaged to blend into the summer landscape. Others, like the red squirrel, establish territories that they aggressively defend. Bighorn sheep have specialized hooves to climb precipitous rock outcroppings.

The snow finds animals like marmots and bears prepared for long slumber having built layers of fat during summer. Other animals such as squirrels, beaver, and pikas are adapted to store food in or near their winter homes. Both the ptarmigan and the snowshoe hare turn white. This adaptation allows them to venture forth for food in winter with protective coloring.

Rocky Mountain National Park is famous for its iconic animals, fit to survive in what we consider a harsh, unique environment.

Chipmunks
Tamias spp.

Few sights are more delightful than a chipmunk sitting on a rock with forepaws folded against its chest.

Chipmunk, NPS photo, Jacob W. Frank

These affable squirrels belong to the genus *Tamias*, which means "storer" in Greek. They hoard food in underground caches for future meals. During winter dormancy, from November to April, they awaken briefly to feed on their larder. Seeds not eaten often germinate, helping to regenerate the forest.

Chipmunks are an important prey for owls, hawks, foxes, coyotes, and bobcats. If they avoid predators, they can live up to 6 years in the park.

Best Places to See Chipmunks

Chipmunk habitat includes rocky areas from shrub-land elevations to above timberline. They are accustomed to people, so you will see them around buildings, campgrounds, and turnouts.

Golden-mantled Ground Squirrel
Callospermophilus lateralis

"It's 'Chip and Dale!'" Well, yes and no. The Disney animators who drew the beloved cartoon characters must have thought that goldenmantled ground squirrels were chipmunks. They are not, but are often misidentified as chipmunks (chipmunks have eye stripes). You will see these endearing squirrels throughout Rocky. They are accustomed to sharing their habitat with humans, and are common denizens around buildings, at scenic turnouts, in campgrounds, and at picnic areas. These loveable ground squirrels will beg for your food, and raid your daypack to loot morsels.

Golden-mantled ground squirrel, NPS photo, Ann Schonlau

Golden-mantled ground squirrels that live at high elevations enter their dens fat on seeds, insects, and bird eggs in late August. September is the time for those living in lower elevations to enter their 8-month hibernation. Their scientific name, *Callospermophilus*, is Greek for *kallos* "beauty," *spermatos* "seed," and *phileo*, "love."

Best Places to See Golden-mantled Ground Squirrels

Golden-mantled ground squirrels are common at all campgrounds and picnic areas. Also look for them in rocky areas at roadside pullouts and along trails.

Wyoming Ground Squirrel
Spermophilus elegans

Rocky Mountain's Rip Van Winkle enters its burrow in August and hibernates until the following March or April. You will see these pudgy, pear-shaped ground squirrels only during the summer months. Even then, the squirrels stay in their burrows at night and during the heat of summer days. The burrow is the center of a ground squirrel's activity. Their physiology

Wyoming ground squirrel, NPS archive

changes midsummer as their bodies begin to process their diet of grasses and leaves, to be stored as fat. Fresh plants become scarce as the season advances, and they may turn to insects and bird's eggs for sustenance.

With litters as large as 11, Wyoming ground squirrels overpopulate an area to the benefit of snakes, coyotes, foxes, badgers, weasels, and hawks. Predators take a toll on the ground squirrels and so do automobiles.

Best Places to See Wyoming Ground Squirrels
The species occupies montane and subalpine ecosystems in Rocky Mountain. It prefers open sagebrush, grasslands, and subalpine meadows.

Red Squirrel
Tamiasciurus hudsonicus

Red squirrel, Alan Leftridge

Also called pine squirrels or chickarees, these forest acrobats will please you with their endearing antics as they leap from branch to branch, tree to tree. You may detect pine squirrels by sound before sight. Their noisy chattering, stomping feet, and vocal scolding are warnings for intruders to stay away. With a home range of less than two soccer fields and populations of two squirrels to three acres, their territories often overlap. They fight rivals to guard their food supplies. Red squirrels do not hibernate, and can live 10 years if they can avoid owls, martens, foxes, and bobcats.

Best Places to See Red Squirrels
Red squirrels are common throughout the park in Douglas-fir, Engelmann spruce, and lodgepole pine communities up to the timberline.

ANIMAL GROUPS

Ever think about what groups of animals are called? Here is a list of the proper collective nouns:

- A gang of moose
- A herd of elk
- A herd of deer
- A sloth of bears
- A colony of beaver
- A pack of wolves
- A knot of toads
- A flight of hawks
- A hover of trout
- A charm of hummingbirds
- An army of frogs
- An unkindness of ravens
- A trip of mountain goats
- A flock of bighorn sheep
- A dray of squirrels
- An earth of foxes
- A paddling of ducks (swimming)
- A team of ducks (flying)
- A murder of crows

Pika
Ochotona princeps

You will hear pikas before you see them. Their short bugle-like squeaks are a warning cry when you approach their territory. When you see pikas, you may agree that they are the cutest, cuddliest-looking, most charismatic inhabitants of the park. Once you locate an animal, look for haystacks. Pikas harvest alpine flowers, sedges, and grasses, then lay them in a cross-hatch pattern over rocks to dry. They scurry to hide their harvest if it begins to rain, then bring the food out to dry once more in the sun.

Pika, NPS photo, Ann Schonlau

Also called rock rabbits, they live near timberline in the rocky crevices that edge alpine meadows. Listen for their bugle and look for these little furballs, the size of a grapefruit with tiny ears and no visible tail. Pikas do not hibernate, but stay active all winter among the rocks, in the dark, under several feet of snow.

Best Places to See Pikas

Listen for pikas as you walk the trails at and above treeline. When you hear one's high-pitch bugle, stop, stand still, and scan for movement among the rocks. Although the bugle is a warning signal, pikas are curious and often reveal themselves if not startled.

PIKAS IN PERIL

Pika, NPS photo, Beth Honea

Pikas live in a narrow temperature range. Insulated by snowpack covering their alpine homes, they can survive the winters without hibernating. If they are exposed to summer temperatures exceeding 70°F for just a few hours, they will perish. Global warming has affected pikas in western states, with a reduction of up to 40 percent of their habitat in some areas. Pikas adjust to these conditions by attempting to relocate up the mountains to climes that are more hospitable. They have already migrated to the highest elevations in the park, with no new territory to enter.

Snowshoe Hare
Lepus americanus

Snowshoe hare, NPS photo, Ann Schonlau

Snowshoe hares are a bit larger than rabbits, with bigger feet and taller ears. Their ears help them detect the sounds of danger, while their muscular bodies and big feet propel them from predators. Although agile and swift, they often cannot evade every fox, bobcat, coyote, owl, or hawk. Their life expectancy in the wild is about one year.

Like their rabbit cousins, snowshoe hares can have two or three litters each year, with one to eight young per litter. Their species must be prolific to keep populations healthy.

Snowshoe hares feed at night, following well-traveled forest paths. Their summer diet includes tree saplings, shrubs, grasses, and flowers. Tree bark and woody plant twigs sustain them in the winter.

The longer daylight hours of spring activate the production of melatonin in hair follicles, leading to the browns and grays of the summer camouflage. The waning daylight hours of autumn stop melatonin creation, leading to the absence of hair color production—and winter white.

Best Places to See Snowshoe Hares

Snowshoe hares can be challenging to see because they are mostly nocturnal and well camouflaged. Watch for them at dawn and dusk along forest trails. In winter, look for their big-footed tracks in the snow.

Yellow-bellied Marmot
Marmota flaviventris

Yellow-bellied marmot, NPS photo, Beth Honea

About the size of a soccer ball, the yellow-bellied marmot is the largest member of the squirrel family. Also known as rockchucks, an adult weighs up to 10 pounds. They are at home in valleys and foothills near rocky outcroppings, where you might discover them performing their mock boxing matches, nuzzling each other, sun bathing (up to 40 percent of their time on a sunny day), and making loud chirping whistles. Summers are time for feasting on grasses, sedges, glacier lilies, paintbrush plants, and silky lupines. Marmots need copious fat to survive the long high-country winter. Early autumn brings cold weather and food scarcity that triggers hibernation. Marmots enter their dens for the final time in September. They hibernate in colonies of 6 to 8, under the rocks and snow for up to 34 weeks.

Best Places to See Yellow-bellied Marmots
Look for marmots at Forest Canyon Overlook and the Rock Cut pullout along Trail Ridge Road.

Bighorn Sheep
Ovis canadensis

Imagine running headlong into a solid wall. Consider doing that every minute for up to 24 hours! Male bighorn sheep do something similar every autumn as they pair off a few feet apart, rear up on their hind legs, and ram each other. You could not endure such a pounding, but the sheep's thick, bony skulls and stout horns prevent serious damage.

Bighorn rams, NPS photo, Ann Schonlau

Their horns represent status and are used as weapons in battles for dominance or mating rights. The bony outgrowth can weigh 30 pounds, more than all the bones in a ram's body. Consider lifting that weight repeatedly for hours. The thin alpine air can carry the crack of their colliding horns a mile away. The battle rages until an adversary leaves.

The park is home to this Colorado state animal. Their split rough hooves are adapted to gripping rocks, allowing them to travel over rugged mountain surfaces. Although their hearing and sense of smell are relatively poor, their eyesight is excellent. The cold of the extreme altitudes does not bother them, for they have a dense coat of gray-brown hair (not wool). Bighorn sheep prefer rock-strewn meadows, making them vulnerable to mountain lions and coyotes. Golden eagles prey on lambs that are born on secluded rock ledges. If they avoid predators, bighorn sheep can live up to 15 years in the park.

The Best of Rocky

ANTLERS OR HORNS?

Horns on a bighorn ram, NPS photo   Antlers in velvet on bull moose, NPS photo, Russell Smith

You may hear westerners refer to elk antlers as horns. This regional vernacular persists. Antlers are bony substances that grow on the heads of male deer, elk, and moose each year. The annual cycle of antler growth is regulated by the lengthening daylight hours in spring. New antlers are covered in fuzzy skin called velvet. Antlers harden by late summer and the velvet peels away. By September, bone-like antlers aid males during competitions of the rut or mating season. Antlers fall off in late winter and the cycle begins again.

Horns are bony outgrowths on the heads of certain ungulates including bighorn sheep. Both males and females have horns. Horns are never shed, but remain with the animal for life.

Best Places to See Bighorn Sheep

Look for bighorn sheep from Sheep Lakes Overlook along the Trail Ridge Road. Scan the meadow with binoculars. You may see them across the river, or on the hillside across the road. Listen for the crack of their horns in autumn.

Mule Deer
Odocoileus hemious

Few animals provide as majestic a sight as a mule deer buck with a large antler rack. That may be why Disney selected the mule deer as the model for Bambi.

Mule deer are browsers, and are the most frequently seen large animals in the park. They have adapted to living near people and their numbers continue to increase in many parts of the country. They are accustomed to vehicle traffic, so you may see them feeding in the meadows as you tour the roads. If one is frightened you'll witness its distinctive bouncing gait as it flees danger.

Mule deer can live a dozen years in the park if they evade mountain lions and automobiles, and if as fawns they are lucky enough to avoid detection by coyotes, eagles, bears, and bobcats.

Mule deer doe and fawn, NPS photo, Ann Schonlau

The challenging winters of the Rocky Mountains also exact a toll on their numbers.

Best Places to See Mule Deer

Look for mule deer browsing in open, shrubby areas around dusk and dawn. During summer, male mule deer range above treeline, while females favor meadows at lower elevations.

Elk
Cervus elaphus nelsoni

If you see something that looks like an oversized deer with a beige rump and legs

> **ANIMAL SPEEDS**
> *The following are maximum speeds of a few animals found in Rocky Mountain National Park. Some can be sustained over long distances, while others are short sprinting speeds.*
> - *Red squirrel: 12 mph*
> - *Black bear: 33 mph*
> - *Mule deer: 35 mph*
> - *Moose: 36 mph*
> - *Snowshoe rabbit: 38 mph*
> - *Coyote: 43 mph*
> - *Elk: 45 mph*
>
> **In Contrast . . .**
> - *The maximum driving speed in the park is 45 mph.*
> - *The fastest Olympic sprinter can run 27 mph.*
>
> *You could outrun a red squirrel, if you were an Olympic sprinter!*

darker than the rest of its body, you are looking at an elk. Also known as wapiti, they are a member of the deer family that includes mule deer, white-tailed deer, moose, and caribou. Before Columbus arrived in the Western Hemisphere, there were more than 10 million elk in North America. Uncontrolled hunting and land development reduced their numbers until various wildlife policies instituted in the 1900s stopped the decline. Today there are about 1 million elk in the lower 48 states. Rocky has a stable population of 600

Bull elk with harem, NPS photo, Ann Schonlau

From spring through summer, one female leads each herd of cows. A cow can weigh up to 500 pounds. Antlers on a 1,100-pound bull can grow up to 5 feet long and weigh 40 pounds. An elk's top two canine teeth are called ivories. Scientists believe ivories are remnants of saber-like tusks that ancestral species of elk used in combat.

to 800. They can live up to 15 years, feeding on grasses, lichens, bushes, tree bark, and saplings.

Visit the park in autumn during mating season to hear bull elk "bugle." At dusk and dawn, they whistle a challenge to other males and, in turn, attract females.

Best Places to See Elk

Summer is a difficult time to see elk because they travel in small groups in the forests. Autumn and early spring are the best times to view them. Before winter, they migrate to lower elevations and congregate in herds.

Bull elk, NPS photo, Ann Schonlau

Moose
Alces alces

How can you tell if a moose is full-grown? Measure its tail, of course. A full-grown adult moose only has a 3-inch tail!

It would be a bad idea to measure its tail, however. This largest member of the deer family can be irritable. Moose

Bull moose, NPS photo, Russell Smith

have been known to charge people, horses, cars, snowmobiles, road maintenance machines, and locomotives. Twice I have come face-to-face with an adult moose on a trail. They showed no interest in yielding—but I did.

A moose cannot be confused with any other animal. Full-grown, it's an awkward-looking, mammoth creature that appears as if a committee designed it. Both sexes have an absurd flap of skin and long hair that hangs from the throat. No one knows the purpose of this "bell," or dewlap.

A mature bull can weigh up to 1,000 pounds, stand 5.5 feet at the shoulder, and sport majestic antlers up to 50 inches wide that weigh 60 pounds. They lose their antlers each year. Imagine the amount of energy the animal must need to grow a new set.

Moos is an Algonquin word that means "twig-eater." An Algonquin legend says that if you dream of moose often, you will live a very long time. Pleasant dreams!

Best Places to See Moose

Look for moose in the Kawuneeche Valley, north of Onahu Creek Trailhead, on the Onahu Creek Trail, and along the Colorado River next to Timber Creek Campground.

MOOSE

Cow and newborn moose, Colorado River, NPS photo, Beth Honea

Moose have hollow hair that helps them float and swim at 6 mph for up to 2 hours. When necessary, moose can dive 20 feet underwater and stay submerged for more than a minute. They can run up to 36 mph for short distances, or as far as 15 miles without stopping. Moose have front teeth only on the bottom jaw. They eat about 40 to 60 pounds of willow, aspen, and aquatic plants a day.

Coyote
Canis latrans

"Barking dog" is the meaning of the coyote's scientific name. Listen for a chorus which may start at dusk with one coyote yipping. Several more will join, leading to a discordant orchestra of yelps.

Coyotes are numerous and have adapted to every area of the park up to the treeline. They are the largest of the park's dog family and look like a small, lean German shepherd. A scavenger and small animal hunter, they are not well tolerated by other predators. Yet they take advantage of badgers' hunting forays. When badgers enter ground squirrel burrows to hunt spring litters, coyotes will wait at nearby tunnel exits for fleeing squirrels.

Best Places to See Coyotes

Coyotes range widely throughout Rocky. They use our roadways, too. You may

Coyote, NPS photo, Ann Schonlau

encounter a coyote trotting down a road in front of your car. Also watch for them in meadows and along forest edges.

Black Bear
Ursus americanus

Their name is deceiving: black bears can be black, blue-black, cinnamon, brown, or blonde. They evolved in forest environments and are excellent tree climbers. They are also solitary, wandering territories of anywhere from 10 to 250 square miles searching for food. Considered opportunistic eaters, their diet includes grasses, roots, nuts, berries, insects, fish, and small mammals. Black bears are extremely adaptable and can develop a preference for human foods and garbage. Bears who become habituated to human food can become aggressive.

Black bear, NPS photo, Ann Schonlau

When autumn snows arrive, black bears seek a cave, a burrow, or a tree cavity to make their dens. They have also been known to find shelter in crawl spaces under buildings. They pass the winter in a state of dormancy, awakening for various reasons, and leaving their den for brief periods. Black bears pass long winters living off body weight that they amassed by gorging on high-energy food all summer and fall. Huckleberries are critical to their health, supplying great amounts of sugar that turns to fat.

Two or three blind, helpless cubs are born in mid-winter and nurse in the den until spring. Mother and cubs will stay together for about 2 years. Black bear life expectancy in the wild is 20 years.

Best Places to See a Black Bear

You can see black bears anywhere in the park. As you drive, check your rearview mirror often. I have seen many black bears running across the road behind my car. You may miss seeing them, but they have likely seen you.

Mountain lion, NPS photo, WL Miller

Mountain Lion
Puma concolor

These solitary, secretive, and seldom seen animals are known by various names, including cougar, puma, catamount, painter, and panther. Common in the park, they blend with their surroundings when they sense humans, eyeing our movements. Their preferred habitat is wooded areas, where they can sneak up on prey. These big cats are strict carnivores that prey on mule deer, elk, and small mammals. Young, old, and weak prey are the most vulnerable to attack. Mountain lions do not make a den, but continually move about their home range of up to 100 square miles in search of food.

Where You Might See a Mountain Lion

These big cats are rarely seen, but a chance sighting could occur anywhere in the park. If you do see a mountain lion, it will likely be from your car while the cat is crossing the road. They are easy to identify: with a tail as long as the rest of its body, the animal takes up half the width of the roadway.

ROCKY'S MAMMALS CHECKLIST

Many of the 70 species of mammals in Rocky Mountain National Park are abundant. You may encounter about 20 of these species. Start a checklist. It could require several visits to the park to see all of these animals, giving you an excuse to return often.

- _____ Chipmunk
- _____ Red Squirrel
- _____ Mountain Lion
- _____ Golden-mantled Ground Squirrel
- _____ Wyoming Ground Squirrel
- _____ Pika
- _____ Bighorn Sheep
- _____ Snowshoe Hare
- _____ Yellow-bellied Marmot
- _____ Beaver
- _____ Mule Deer
- _____ Rocky Mountain Elk
- _____ Moose
- _____ Coyote
- _____ Black Bear

BEST PLACES TO SEE WILDLIFE FROM THE ROAD

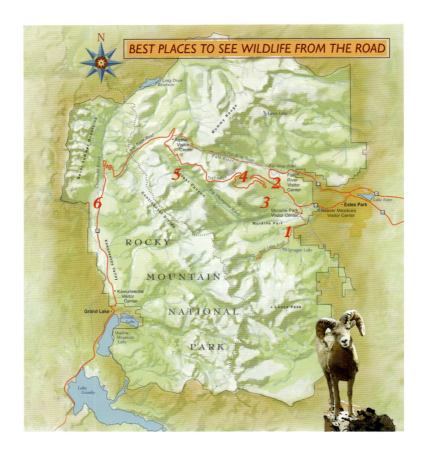

Volunteer Bighorn Brigade, NPS photo, Beth Honea

Where can you see wildlife in Rocky? Anytime and any place. Wildlife wanders these mountains and meadows throughout the year, but there are specific places you can expect to see certain animals. Every autumn, elk herds congregate in the meadows

Best Places to See Wildlife from the Road

for their annual ritual in which the males battle for harems. Mule deer are common and gather in smaller numbers near forest margins. Coyotes, foxes, bobcats, and raptors are attracted to places where they find squirrels, rabbits, and other small mammals. Black bears seek late summer berries in brushy meadows. Knowing the habitat in which animals are likely found increases your chances of seeing them.

Here are probable places to see particular animals from the road.

1. **Moraine Park:** elk, mule deer
2. **Horseshoe Park:** bighorn sheep, elk
3. **Many Parks Curve:** chipmunks, golden-mantled ground squirrels
4. **Rainbow Curve:** chipmunks, golden-mantled ground squirrels
5. **Rock Cut:** yellow-bellied marmots
6. **Kawuneeche Valley:** moose, elk

Near Sheep Lakes, NPS photo, Ann Schonlau

NOTABLE INSECTS

When you think of Rocky Mountain National Park's iconic animals, you probably do not consider insects. Although you might view some of them as nuisances, they play vital roles in the park's ecology. Unimaginable numbers of insects pollinate most of Rocky's wildflowers, trees, and shrubs, and are an integral part of forest succession through infestation. They are also necessary food for countless birds, reptiles, fish, and mammals. Many of these insects migrate during part of their lifecycles beyond the park, drawing attention to Rocky as a wildland and habitat larger than its political boundaries.

Arctic blue butterfly, NPS photo, Jim Westfall

A Superabundance of Butterflies.

The National Park Service has confirmed 141 butterfly species in the park, representing five major families. You might see hundreds of butterflies during your visit. How can you tell them apart? Here are seven common butterflies that you might encounter, and where you could see them.

BRUSHFOOTS (FAMILY NYMPHALIDAE)

Brushfoots are perhaps the most beloved family of butterflies because of their bright color patterns, large sizes, and common sightings. The family includes the monarch, viceroy, morning cloak, checkerspots, and fritillaries. They get their name because their first pair of legs have evolved into brush-like appendages, used to taste-test host plants and to clean their mouthparts.

Dotted Checkerspot *(Poladryas minuta)*

You will see checkerspots patrolling around flowers in the afternoons near foothill ridges, in grasslands, and over open mountain meadows from July through mid-August, feeding on the nectar of yellow composite flowers.

Weidemeyer's Admiral *(Limenitis weidemeyerii)*

Males perch on trees and in shrubs watching for females. Look for Weidemeyer's admirals flying in mid- to late summer, patrolling for mates along the Fern Lake and Wild Basin trails.

Green Comma *(Polygonia faunus)*

All comma butterflies have extremely scalloped wing edges. Adults hibernate and mate the following spring. Look for males perching on rocks or plants in gullies in the late afternoon waiting for females to pass.

BLUES AND COPPERS (FAMILY LYCAENIDAE)

These are small or tiny butterflies that hold their wings close to their little bodies when at rest. They have fun group names like elfins, hairstreaks, blues, and coppers.

Ruddy Copper *(Lycaena rubidus monachensis)*
Look for ruddy coppers in July and August in montane and lower subalpine habitats. Other members of the family in the park include elfins and hairstreaks.

SWALLOWTAILS (FAMILY PAPILIONIDAE)

Swallowtails are some of the largest, most popular butterflies. They are recognizable by their trailing tails.

Western Tiger Swallowtail *(Papilio rutulus)*
Look for swallowtails like the western tiger in the montane zone. The males often congregate, along with other species of swallowtails, at pools and along streams and rivers. They drink from the water and mud, extracting minerals and moisture.

WHITES AND SULFURS (FAMILY PIERIDAE)

These butterflies are mostly medium in size and range in color from yellow to orange to white. They bask with their wings closed and rotated toward the sun. Whites and sulfurs are often the first butterflies that you will see in the spring.

Queen Alexandra's Sulphur *(Colias alexandra)*
Look for male Alexandra's sulphur butterflies mud-puddling throughout the warm months in montane and subalpine areas.

SKIPPERS (FAMILY HESPERIIDAE)

These medium-size butterflies fly in a skipping motion. When they are at rest, you can identify them by their hooked antennae. Most of the species in the park are small and earth-toned, blending well into their resting places.

Snow's Skipper *(Paratrytone snowi)*
Adults have a very swift flight. Males perch in gullies all day to wait for females. Look for Snow's skippers in the openings in ponderosa pine forests and along the streams and gulches of montane meadows.

Other Insects

Mayflies, stoneflies, salmonflies, and caddisflies are groups of aquatic insects that are critical to Rocky's ecology. They feed on plant matter that falls into rivers and streams, breaking down and redistributing the nutrients for other organisms. A great variety of terrestrial, flying, and aquatic animals prey upon them. And because they are hypersensitive to pollution, scientists monitor their numbers and use the results as a barometer for the ecosystem's health.

The native mountain pine beetle can be found infesting lodgepole, ponderosa, and limber pine forests. Pine beetles burrow through the bark to deposit their eggs. The larvae eat their way around the tree, cutting off the flow of nutrients. Adult mountain pine beetles emerge from the trees in midsummer, leaving exit holes that ooze pitch. The pitch accumulates on the surface in crusty mounds. Look for "pitch tubes" on the pine trees. Infested trees die and their needles turn brown or a rusty red. Such infestations are natural and cyclic. The mass die-off opens the forest to new trees and understory growth. Though the effect on the forest looks drastic, bark beetle outbreaks benefit woodpeckers and other birds that feast on the beetles and their larvae.

Pine bark beetle pitch tube, NPS archives

Mosquitoes abound in Rocky during the warm months. You could find swarms of them in cool, damp areas as well as on warm, sunny hillsides. What are they good for? Mosquitoes are important because they pollinate plants. Only female mosquitoes bite animals. They seek blood protein needed for their eggs to develop. Female mosquitoes are attracted to carbon dioxide. They can sense the carbon dioxide you exhale. Wearing long sleeves, pants, and socks, and tying a bandanna around your neck that has been sprayed with a repellent are most effective for keeping mosquitoes from biting. If you do get a mosquito bite, even with all your precautions, just consider it a vacation souvenir from one of Rocky's infamous insects.

BOREAL TOADS (Bufo boreas)

Boreal toad, NPS archives

These 3- to 5-inch-long chubby toads are inclined to walk rather than hop. The toads are adapted to montane lakes and woods, but they're also found in high-country marshes, ponds, bogs, and quiet shallow water up to 12,000 feet. Considered Colorado's only alpine toad, they are threatened by a disease called chytrid fungus. This globally occurring disease appears to be capable of infecting most of the world's 6,000 amphibian species. The boreal toad is on Colorado's list of endangered species.

BEST WILDFLOWERS

Life is found everywhere, from the bottom of the oceans to boiling hot springs, even on ancient glaciers. Animals and plants thrive throughout the park, even across the expansive alpine tundra, adapted to the conditions that we call intolerable.

August visitors are often surprised to see magnificent wildflower displays along Trail Ridge Road. Why are there so many flowers this late in summer? It makes sense if you think of Rocky Mountain National Park as a "vertical garden."

Generally, every 100-foot gain in elevation delays blooming by about one day. Springtime flowers that bloom around Estes Park in May will open along upper Trail Ridge Road in July. Likewise, flowers opening in late July at lower elevations will blossom a month later in the alpine region.

Most of the flowering plants are perennial. Their roots remain alive but dormant over winter, so plants are ready to grow as the snow melts. Thousands of generations of adaptations have made them precisely acclimated to their habitat. Some have been alive for more than 100 years, undisturbed in this wild area.

The National Park Service estimates there are more than 1,000 species of flowering plants in Rocky Mountain National Park. Iconic wildflowers associated with the park are alpine avens, alpine sunflower, sky pilot, and alpine forget-me-not. Other flowers that provoke wonder in a park visitor are the paintbrush, pasqueflower, and Colorado columbine.

ALPINE TUNDRA WILDFLOWERS

Snow buttercup, NPS photo, Jacob W. Frank

As you travel Trail Ridge Road, you will note that there are no large plants in the tundra. Instead, look for low-growing woody shrubs, mosses, lichens, and compact flowers in plump, round pillow shapes. These are called cushion plants. They are slow-growing perennials that are adapted to the tundra's cold, dry winds, intense sunlight, and nutrient-poor soil. Venture on a walk to marvel at the beauty of these flowers. But please avoid stepping on cushion plants; they are fragile and some are over a century old. The paved Tundra Communities Trail (park at the Rock Cut pullout on Trail Ridge Road) provides alpine access without risk of trampling the vegetation.

Regardless of the month, bring your walking shoes and plan to discover the best of Rocky Mountain National Park's wildflowers. Even the smallest flowers elicit awe.

Alpine Avens
Geum rossii

This familiar looking flower is often mistaken for a buttercup because of its shiny leaves and yellow petals. You may find large patches of alpine avens blooming throughout the summer.

Alpine avens, USDA Forest Service, Don Finnie

August and September finds their leaves gleaming red, bathing the tundra in splashes of color. Pikas harvest and dry alpine avens to store in their winter pantry.

Where You Can Find Alpine Avens
Look for alpine avens near treeline and on alpine tundra.

Snow-lily
Erythronium grandiflorum

Also called glacier lily, these plants generate heat from carbohydrates stored in their roots. The heat melts the overlaying inch or two of snow, allowing the stem to push through and bloom.

Their bulbs are tasty to rodents and bears, while deer, elk, and bighorn sheep eat their seedpods. These delicate plants can withstand a Rocky Mountain winter, but not the weight of even a child's step. The slightest pressure will kill the bulb.

Where You Can Find Snow-lilies

Snow-lily, NPS photo, Ed Austin and Herb Jones

Snow-lilies flourish in remote backcountry areas. They emerge along the edges of snowfields in the subalpine zone as snow melts.

Alpine Sunflower
Rydbergia grandiflora

The heads of most sunflower species track the sun, but not so with the alpine sunflower. Instead, these flower heads always face east. At high altitude, the sunflowers grow so close to the ground that their leaves and stems become hidden by the profusion of blossoms. The harsh conditions in which they thrive require this perennial to live several decades before the plant has stored enough energy to bloom. Afterward, it creates its seeds and dies.

Alpine sunflowers, NPS photo, Ann Schonlau

Where You Can Find Alpine Sunflowers
Alpine sunflowers bloom June through August in alpine meadows.

Heartleaf Arnica
Arnica cordifolia

Arnica is a Greek word that refers to the resemblance of the soft hairy leaves to a lamb's ears. Heartleaf arnica plants are important in the life cycles of many butterfly and moth species, as their larvae feed on the leaves. The best growing conditions allow them to form a loose carpet of cheery, bright flowers in shady, moist areas.

Where You Can Find Heartleaf Arnica
Look for this perennial blooming in moist, rich soil at montane elevations starting in June. By mid-July, you will find its colorful displays in the subalpine.

Heartleaf arnica, NPS photo, Jacob W. Frank

Colorado Columbine
Aquilegia coerulea

Colorado columbine, NPS photo, Walt Kaesler

Colorado's state flower grows at almost every elevation in the vertical landscape of Rocky Mountain National Park. This perennial has plenty of cousins. There are 60 to 70 species growing in North America. The common name columbine comes from Latin for "dove." Someone imagined the resemblance of five doves clustered together in the inverted flower. The long spurs of the flower contain nectar, which attracts butterflies and bees.

Where You Can Find Columbine
You will find Colorado columbine blooming from June through August in lower-elevation woodlands, alpine areas, subalpine forests, and rocky alpine sites.

Alpine Forget-me-not
Eritrichum aretioides

Alpine forget-me-not, NPS photo, Jacob W. Frank

This dwarf alpine cushion plant is one of the first to bloom on the tundra. There are several flowers on the plant, with each on a stem about an inch tall. Their fragrant, delicate beauty makes you wonder how forget-me-nots have adapted to survive the cold and storms of their high mountain habitat.

Where You Can Find Alpine Forget-me-nots
Look for alpine forget-me-nots blooming from June to July in open rocky alpine slopes and dry meadows.

Pasqueflower
Pulsatilla patens

Pasqueflower, NPS photo, Jacob W. Frank

The discovery of a curious looking mass of silvery fluff on an 18-inch stalk brings wonder to visitors unfamiliar with this member of the buttercup family. It has several other names such as wild crocus, prairie crocus, and Easter flower. The twisting mass in the feathery plumed heads contains the seeds. The flower—a large, pale purple cup with a yellow center—bloomed long ago, as early as March at lower elevations. Pasqueflower is the official flower of South Dakota and Manitoba.

Where You Can Find Pasqueflowers
Pasqueflowers prefer the foothills and open slopes of the montane zone.

Sky Pilot
Polemonium viscosum

You may regret disturbing this plant. *Viscosum* means "sticky," and if you step on a sky pilot you will learn why it is also known as skunkweed. The odor will remain on your shoes for several hours. Sky pilots growing at higher elevations tend to smell sweeter.

Where You Can Find Sky Pilots
Sky pilots bloom from June to early August in alpine meadows up to the highest elevations of the park. Look for them in protected rock crevices.

Sky pilot, NPS photo

Mountain Harebell
Campanula rotundifolia

The name harebell comes from European folklore. Some people once believed that harebells grew in places that hares lived and that witches used its flower juices to change themselves into hares.

This delicate-looking flower is in fact quite hardy. Harebell grows throughout Rocky Mountain National Park and in mountainous areas around the world. It is adapted to a variety of habitats and can be found in full sun or shade, dry or moist soils, and in forests, meadows, cliffs, and lake beaches, as well as sprouting in roadside gravel.

Mountain harebell, NPS photo, Jacob W. Frank

Where You Can Find Harebells

Harebells bloom from late June into September everywhere, from the lowest montane elevations to alpine tundra.

Mountain lupine, NPS photo

Mountain Lupine
Lupinus argenteus

Botanists believed that this ubiquitous perennial devoured soil nutrients and so gave it the name *Lupinus*, Latin for wolf. Further research proved that lupine plants preferred poor soil, rather than made it. The plant works with mycorrhizal fungi to create the soil nutrients it needs. Ground squirrels eat the leaves and flowers. Bighorn sheep feed on the dead leaves and stems in the winter. After a rain or morning dew, look for the small droplet of water in the center of each leaf.

Where You Can Find Lupine

Lupine prefers dry montane to subalpine areas. Look for the flowers—which may be blue, purple, pink, or (rarer) white—in June and July along road cuts and in rocky, open meadows.

Fairy Slipper
Calypso bulbosa

This perennial is also known as calypso orchid. Both names suggest its delicate beauty. They live no more than five years, many dying earlier because they are susceptible to disturbance. Walk cautiously among them. A footstep kills.

Fairy slipper, NPS photo, Ann Schonlau

Where You Can Find Fairy Slippers
Look for fairy slippers blooming during late spring in cool, deep-shaded, moist montane forests.

Fireweed
Chamerion danielsii

Fireweed is a fast-growing, pioneer perennial that colonizes disturbed areas by seeds and spreading roots. Native in the northern hemisphere, it became known as *bombweed* in Europe due to its rapid colonization of bomb craters during World War II. The plant can grow to 4 feet tall after it establishes in burnt areas, clear-cuts, and along roadsides. Fireweed adds nutrients to the soil essential for plant succession. Some people make jellies and syrups from the blossoms.

Where You Can Find Fireweed
Fireweed blooms from July to September in montane and subalpine forests, meadows, and disturbed areas.

Fireweed, NPS photo, Jacob W. Frank

Shooting Star
Dodecatheon pulchellum

Shooting stars are "buzz pollinators." They release pollen from their stamens only from violent shaking. There is no landing platform for insects. A visiting bumblebee must cling to the flower, thus releasing the pollen with its vibrating wings.

Where You Can Find Shooting Stars
Expect to find shooting stars in wet areas in the montane zone in early June, and through July in wet subalpine meadows.

Paintbrush
Castilleja miniata

Shooting star, NPS photo, Jacob W. Frank

The Wyoming state flower is found in many colors, including red, orange, and white. It appears yellow in the tundra due to the absence of iron in the soil. This showy perennial is named for its colorful, ragged bracts that appear to have been dipped in paint. Hummingbirds seek its nectar, leading some botanists to theorize that paintbrush plants and hummingbirds co-evolved.

Where You Can Find Paintbrush
Paintbrush plants grow best in moist soil. Look for their bright colors painting montane meadows and subalpine areas to treeline.

Paintbrush, NPS photo, Jacob W. Frank

PAINTBRUSH Castilleja spp.

Texas folklore tells of Little Gopher, a child who was unhappy because he is not good at running, shooting, or riding and would never be a brave. He fears that he will amount to little until a shaman tells him that everyone has something to contribute. Someday he will learn what he offers.

Several years later, Little Gopher has a dream-vision during which he is told that he will record the events of his tribe for his people to remember. He is shown what he needs to paint the stories, but he realizes that he misses the vibrant colors needed to show the sunset. One night, he receives another vision that the paints that he needs will be provided on a hilltop the next morning. Arriving at the spot, he finds brushes of all colors sticking up from the ground. He paints the most beautiful sunset and leaves the brushes on the hill. The next day, the People find that the brushes have rooted and turned into the paintbrush plants that we now enjoy.

Paintbrush, Upper Ouzel Trail, NPS photo, Crystal Brindle

BEST TREES

You might be awed by the many varieties of conifer trees in Rocky Mountain National Park. Or they may all look alike. Here is one characteristic of each of the iconic species to help you identify what you are seeing.

- If it has jigsaw-like bark, it's a ponderosa pine.
- If it looks like you could make a log cabin of it, it's a lodgepole pine.
- If it appears blue, it's a Colorado blue spruce.
- If the slender limbs appear long and bendable, it's a limber pine.
- If it has cones that point upward like candles, it's a subalpine fir.
- If the top of the tree has a narrow point, it's an Engelmann spruce.
- If its characteristics don't match any of the above, it's probably a Douglas-fir.

Rocky Mountain National Park's trees live in two major ecosystems: the montane and the subalpine.

The montane ecosystem occurs at the lowest elevations of the park to about 9,500 feet. The ecosystem is characterized by dry, south-facing slopes with ponderosa pine, and cool, moist north-facing slopes supporting Douglas-fir, lodgepole pine, ponderosa pine, some Engelmann spruce, and groves of quaking aspens.

The subalpine ecosystem lies above the montane up to the treeline. Characteristic trees include subalpine fir, Engelmann spruce, and limber pine.

Ponderosa Pine
Pinus ponderosa

It seems like ponderosa pine trees have a plan to keep other trees from growing in their forest. Fire benefits ponderosa pine communities by removing plants and trees that compete for water and nutrients. They shed masses of needles that, once dried, burn with ease. Their thick bark and few lower branches protect mature ponderosas from ground fires.

Ponderosa pine, NPS photo, Walt Kaesler

WILDLIFE SKYSCRAPERS

You will see many dead trees as you travel through the park. Fires, insects, and various diseases have killed these trees. Dead trees are important to the ecology of a forest. Dead standing trees are called snags, an old Scandinavian word for "stump of a tree."

The tallest snags provide the best animal shelter. These "skyscraper" environments limit predator access to roosting and nesting wildlife. Look about you as you travel through the park . . . how many wildlife skyscrapers do you see?

Red-tailed hawk atop a snag, NPS photo, Ann Schonlau

Wildlife and snags
- Eagles, herons, ospreys, and hawks perch and nest on the tops.
- Woodpeckers and brown thrashers feed on insects.
- Bats roost and birds nest under overhanging loose bark.
- Woodpeckers, nuthatches, wood ducks, owls, pine martens, and squirrels nest in snag cavities.
- Nationwide, 85 percent of all bird species use snags for nesting, shelter, or food.

Find trees with jigsaw puzzle-like bark colored gray, red, or yellowish. Ancient trees are sometimes called yellowbellies. Sniff the bark of a large pine. Can you detect a fragrance? Some people note a vanilla or a butterscotch scent.

Lodgepole Pine
Pinus contorta

Pinus contorta ("contorted pine") is a scientific name that contradicts the straight appearance of these trees. Botanists who first identified the characteristics of lodgepole pine were studying specimens growing on the Pacific Coast. There, the tree's growth pattern is affected by salt air and wind, causing them to twist and bend. Shore pine is the common name on the coast. It was several years later when botanists learned that shore pine and lodgepole pine were genetically identical. Nonetheless, the species retains its confusing scientific name.

Lodgepole pines evolved as a fire-dependent species. Most of their cones are covered in a wax that won't melt below 130°F, only then releasing the seeds. They are the first coniferous tree seeds to germinate following a fire. Without competition from other species, and with a fertile bed for seedlings, the trees reach for the sun. In the Rocky Mountain West, lodgepole pine trees grow straight enough to use the long trunks for construction. You'll see lodgepole pines framing tepee lodges, cabins, and homes.

Lodgepole pine, NPS photo

Limber Pine
Pinus flexilis

Both its common name and scientific name refer to its bendable quality. Young limbs are so pliable they can be tied into knots (but please don't). Limber pine grows near the treeline, enduring the onslaught of inhospitable weather. Look for clusters of

Limber pine, NPS photo

limber pine gracing the edges of lakes and rocky outcrops, where other species struggle to exist. They tend to be large-diameter trees that look like ancient sentinels.

Engelmann Spruce
Picea engelmannii

The trees you see in the subalpine forests include Engelmann spruce. They can survive in the highest and the coldest areas of the park, tolerating -50°F. The smallness of the trees belies their age; they are stunted in the extreme conditions and even small trees can be several hundred years old.

In contrast to Engelmann spruce trees that live in the subalpine zone, at lower elevations, especially along creek bottoms, this species can grow to 150 feet tall over the span of 400 years. Here, they can be just as blue as the Colorado blue spruce.

Colorado Blue Spruce
Picea pungens

Young blue spruce needles have a silvery blue cast, providing a color that renders the species worthy of State Tree status. Older wild trees are just green.

Engelmann spruce, NPS photo

Colorado blue spruce cone, USDA NRCS photo, D. E. Herman

Colorado blue spruce are not common in the park. They grow on moist slopes and along streams. Outside of the park, many homeowners love this tree as a landscaping accent. Horticulturists propagate the species to take advantage of the bluish tendencies, giving this symmetrical shaped tree several ornamental varieties.

Subalpine Fir
Abies lasiocarpa

A popular Christmas tree, subalpine firs can withstand Rocky Mountain National Park's coldest temperatures. Heavy snow loads press trunks and lower branches to the ground, where they root and perpetuate the "krummholz" growth pattern.

Douglas-fir
Pseudotsuga menziesii

Despite what everyone calls it, the Douglas-fir is not a true fir. Its scientific name declares that it is a false *(pseudo)*

Subalpine fir, NPS photo

KRUMMHOLZ FORMATIONS AND FLAGGING

Winter tempests blast through rock gaps high atop ridges at speeds approaching 200 mph. It seems unimaginable that trees could live in this hostile environment—but they do. Picturesque in their distorted shapes, the sculpted, sandblasted, diminutive forms misrepresent their ages. Limber pine, subalpine fir, and Engelmann spruce trees endure here; many are hundreds of years old.

Krummholz, NPS photo, RG Johnsson

Exposure to extreme wind, cold, and dryness near treeline causes trees to be stunted, twisted, and shaped into elfin-like tree stands, or krummholz (German for "crooked wood"). A tree seed sprouts on the downwind side of a rock. Eventually, the shoot grows tall and is no longer protected by the rock formation. The shoot dies in the bitter drying winds. The tree survives by extending growth sideways. Huddled behind the rock, the tree adds trunk girth and new limbs downwind. In time, its own wood begins to shelter newer growth. The tree can now expand away from the protection of the rock formation. New tree seeds will eventually germinate on the leeward side of the tree, and will some day form a small grove of dwarfish trees.

Flagging due to wind, Alan Leftridge

A variation on a krummholz formation is a flagged tree. Branches on the windward side are killed or deformed by icy winds that destroy new growth, giving the tree a characteristic flag-like appearance. The lower portion of the tree is often protected by snow and lacks the flagging. Whereas krummholz trees grow in small groups, flagged trees often grow alone, self-portraits in a violently sculpted world.

hemlock *(tsuga)*. Douglas-fir trees are found throughout the park, and form dense forests on northern slopes. The trees are critical to wildlife diets in Rocky Mountain National Park. The profuseness of Douglas-fir cones provides a feast for red squirrels, chipmunks, and countless insects that devour the seeds before the cones open.

Douglas-fir cone, NPS photo, Christine Duchesne

Quaking Aspen
Populus tremuloides

Look for dome-shaped groves of deciduous trees throughout the park. These are made of quaking aspens, the most widely distributed tree species in North America. Their wind-scattered seeds can travel great distances. Once established in moist and disturbed areas, the seedlings become pioneer trees. Thereafter, they propagate by their roots outward, with the older trees in the center. The leaves of these genetically identical tree islands turn a brilliant yellow and orange each autumn, painting the Rocky Mountains with liquid sunshine.

Quaking aspen, NPS photo, Ann Schonlau

BEST ACTIVITIES FOR CHILDREN

Rocky Mountain National Park was set aside for everyone, not just adults. Here is a list of activities you can do with your children to increase their awareness, reveal its wonders, and build lasting memories of Rocky.

Child exploring park relief map, Fall River Visitor Center, NPS photo, Katy Sykes

Special Programs

Explore, learn, and protect as a Junior Ranger! Go to romo_junior_ranger@nps.gov before your visit to get information about Rocky Mountain National Park's Junior Ranger Program. It is designed to encourage your children to explore the park at their own pace. Children attend a ranger-led program and complete at least five activities in a Junior Ranger booklet. Rocky Mountain National Park Junior Ranger badges are awarded when a park ranger checks their finished booklet. Booklets are available for ages 5 and up. Get them at the Junior Ranger Headquarters located at the Moraine Park Discovery Center. Your child can also participate online at the National Park Service's WebRangers site: www.nps.gov/webrangers/.

Go on a Photo Safari

Put that smartphone or digital camera to a good educational use. Help your kids organize their photos into a story about their vacation or day-hike. Select a theme like, "Patterns of Rocky Mountain National Park." Help your child to see and capture images of patterns, such as patterns in plant growth, types of flowers, tree leaves, where animals are found, lichen growth, clouds and weather, and people movement. Encourage them to post their story on their favorite social media site. Want a theme other than Patterns? Possibilities abound—Change, Adaptation, Interdependence, Similarities, Differences—or think of your own theme.

Attend an Evening Program

Kids love attending evening programs. Help them learn about the fascinating diversity of Rocky Mountain National Park with the help of an experienced park ranger. Topics include bears, birds, history, climate change, and geology. Presentations are at the following campgrounds: Aspenglen, Glacier Basin, Moraine Park, and Timber Creek. Auditorium programs are held at the Kawuneeche Visitor Center and the Beaver Meadows Visitor Center. Check the park newspaper for specific times and locations.

Join in a Ranger-led Hike

The National Park Service offers a variety of ranger-led programs especially designed for youth and families. See the park newspaper distributed at entrance stations and look for Ranger Programs. Child-centered programs are offered at the Holzwarth Historic Site and Kawuneeche Visitor Center.

Junior Ranger Program, NPS photo, Debbie Biddle

Take a Walk in the Park

Do you want to explore the park with your child without a guide? Rocky Mountain National Park has more than 355 miles of trails. Start with short, educational, and exciting walks that will inspire your child to learn. Consider these self-guided trails: Tundra Communities Trail, Bear Lake Nature Trail, Lulu City Trail, Coyote Valley Trail, and Lily Lake Trail.

Want to take on more challenging experiences? Take into account your child's abilities, and consider some unguided short walks, where you and your child can share in the discoveries of Rocky's myriad wonders.

GOOD HIKES FOR KIDS

Lily Lake Area

Lily Ridge Trail, 1.3-mile loop, 240 feet elevation gain.

This is a fun, short hike above and around Lily Lake. Make sure you have some refreshments for the end of the hike. The trail begins and ends in the Lily Lake Picnic Area, where you have a great view of the lake and distant Longs Peak.

Fall River Area

Gem Lake, 3.6 miles round-trip, 1,090 feet elevation gain.

The trail to the lake can seem longer than 1.8 miles and includes several rocky switchbacks. Along the way, you will wind through varied forests with lots of wildflowers. The lake is small and surrounded by boulders.

Bear Lake Area

Sprague Lake, 1-mile loop, no elevation gain.
The level, hard-packed trail is easy walking for the youngest child. Strollers are also allowed. The setting is lovely, with views of the Continental Divide. Take the opportunity to skip rocks easily found along the shore.

Alberta Falls, 1.7 miles round-trip, 160 feet elevation gain.
Make sure that you bring a snack or a picnic lunch. This may be the most popular waterfall in the park. You'll want to linger while your child discovers the sights and sounds of this beautiful spot.

Emerald Lake, 4 miles round-trip, 650 feet elevation gain.
This hike makes a good half-day exploration. The trail passes Bear, Nymph, and Dream Lakes.

Cub Lake, 4.6 miles round-trip, 540 feet elevation gain.
The trail to Cub Lake will delight your child, as you cross the Big Thompson River and travel through fields of wildflowers and aspen forests. Water lilies cover Cub Lake and where they don't, the surrounding mountains are reflected in the water.

The Loch, 6.1 miles round-trip, 730 feet elevation gain.
Consider this a long day-hike for kids, not for the inexperienced. Be sure to bring all the supplies necessary for a full day's exploration. The trail to The Loch has several switchbacks and great views. The Loch is beautiful and there are plenty of places to rest and take in the wonders of the surroundings.

Wild Basin Area

Copeland Falls, 0.9 mile round-trip, 75 feet elevation gain.
This leisurely trail goes directly through the forest, reaching Copeland Falls after about 15 minutes. Explore the area, and find a good place to sit with your child and enjoy the sights, sounds, and smells.

Calypso Cascades, 3.6 miles round-trip, 700 feet elevation gain.
You pass Copeland Falls on your hike to Calypso Cascades. The cascade is named for the pink calypso orchids (fairy slippers) that bloom here in late spring.

Kawuneeche Valley

Adams Falls, 0.9 mile round-trip, 115 feet elevation gain.
This is a short trail with an easy climb to the falls. Little children will feel a sense of accomplishment as they discover that they can succeed in making it to the waterfall. Adams Falls is a popular hike in the valley.

Holzwarth Historic District

Explore with your child the historic dude ranch and homestead of the Holzwarth family. You will find tours, brochures, and signage at the homestead that interprets the site's history.

Read Aloud

Be prepared. A rainy day or a lull in activities gives you an opportunity to read a book with your child. Many entertaining and informative books are available at the Rocky Mountain Conservancy bookstore in Estes Park and at Rocky Mountain Conservancy Nature Stores in the park visitor centers.

Reading about the park, NPS photo, John Marino

Pick some that you want to read and that will give your child a better understanding of Rocky Mountain National Park's heritage.

Plan ahead to build the anticipation phase of your trip. Contact the Rocky Mountain Conservancy (http://rmconservancy.org/shop-rmna), and order books that will delight your child. Read to them as you travel to Rocky. Here are some of the dozens of available books that will enhance a child's experiences in the park:

- *Black Bear Babies* (ages 0-3)
- *Moose Babies* (ages 0-3)
- *Be a Park Ranger,* Robert Rath (ages 2 and up)
- *How Do Bears Sleep?* E. J. Bird (ages 2 and up)
- *The Cutest Critter,* Marion Bauer and Stan Tekiela (ages 2 and up)
- *The Ugly Mooseling,* Linda Olson and Greta Gretzinger (ages 2 and up)

- *Lost in the Woods*, Carl R. Sams II and Jean Stoick (ages 2 and up)
- *Lil' MacDonald Likes to Hike*, Jennifer Taylor Tormalehto (ages 4 and up)
- *A Pika's Tale*, Sally Plumb (ages 4 and up)
- *Color the Wild Rockies*, Mary Pruett (ages 4 and up)
- *Who Pooped in the Park? Rocky Mountain National Park* Gary Robson (ages 5 to 8)
- *A Child's Introduction to the Night Sky*, Michael Driscoll and Meredith Hamilton (ages 8 and up)

Ride a Horse

Give your children a sense of what it must have been like to see Rocky Mountain National Park before automobiles became the primary source of transportation. Rides are one and two hours through forested landscapes. Outfitters offer horseback rides at Moraine Park, and Sprague Lake for those age 8 and older. Several other outfitters operate adjacent to the park.

Reflect

Today's fast-paced, gadget-filled lifestyle is busy with distractions. Rocky Mountain National Park presents wonderful opportunities to take a deep breath and reconnect with the natural world. Find a quiet, peaceful spot. Challenge your child to sit in solitude for 5 or 10 minutes. (Try it yourself!) Ask them to think about what they hear, smell, and see. Encourage them to write or draw about the experience and what their senses revealed to them. As they settle in for the night, ask your child to reflect on what they liked about the day's activities.

View the Night Sky

More than 80 percent of Americans live in cities and suburbs. Living under the glow of urban lights, children do not experience the excitement of seeing the Milky Way, August's Perseids meteor shower, or summer constellations. Rocky Mountain National Park's dark nighttime skies are excellent for stargazing. Do it on your own, or attend one of the Night Sky Programs, offered throughout the summer by park rangers. Hear star stories, identify constellations, and view the night sky through telescopes. The night sky inspires awe to a child and its mysteries are brought to light when a family member takes the time to share in the discovery.

BEST THINGS TO DO ON A RAINY OR SNOWY SUMMER'S DAY

Lawn Lake, NPS photo, Crystal Brindle

Weather can be raw and dramatic in this thin air. That innocent cloud to the west can turn a warm, sunny day into a cold, rainy one in minutes. A bright April morning could end with a snowy afternoon. Accept the drama as a fact of visiting the Backbone of the Continent. Make the most of wild weather with activities such as these:

- Photograph the stormy conditions; they make some of the most interesting images.
- Park in a pullout in Horseshoe Park and watch wildlife from your car. Stormy weather sends most humans indoors, but other animals carry on their outdoor lives.
- Bundle up and take a stroll around Bear Lake or Lily Lake.
- Visit the Artist-in-Residence at the William Allen White cabin in Moraine Park.
- Explore the Moraine Park Discovery Center.
- Spend extra time in the visitor centers, and make sure that you see what's showing in the auditorium.
- Spend extra time at the Alpine Visitor Center where you can shop, have a warm drink, and watch the weather through the large observation windows.

WINTER IN ROCKY

Snowshoers, NPS photo, Jon Olsen

We think of winter weather extremes—lots of snow and bitter temperatures—as a severe winter. Rocky's plants and animals exist in conditions that we consider unbearable. Temperatures can hover around -20°F for several days. But the plants and animals here are well adapted to this climate with its wide weather variations.

Lodgepole pines, subalpine firs, and Engelmann spruce trees are able to withstand sustained temperatures of -40°F. Long-lived perennial grasses and flowers have stored enough nourishment in their roots and stems to survive the dark months. Their energy reserves give them a head start, growing even as winter lingers. Some, like the snow-lily, begin to grow under the snow.

Many animals rest, drifting into hibernation and torpor. Other wildlife remains active beneath the snow or on the surface. Non-hibernating animals are well adapted to conditions we find unlivable. Animals you might see in winter include elk, mule deer, and coyotes, all of which may be seen along the road in Horseshoe Park and Moraine Park. You will not see pikas in winter. They thrive despite frigid temperatures, protected beneath the jumble of rocks and a mantle of snow as they feed on the flowers and forbs they stored for the long winter.

Deep snow may be a problem for us, but not for ptarmigans. Skies clear after a cold front dumps snow, and temperatures can drop to record lows. Ptarmigans react by diving headlong into the fluffy snow and ruffling their feathers to make an air pocket. Their body heat keeps the cavern warm, while a few inches above it may be many degrees colder.

Rocky Mountain National Park is open all year. Trail Ridge Road is closed in winter between Many Parks Curve on the east and the Colorado River Trailhead on the west, but Bear Lake Road provides access to scenic areas and trails throughout winter. One of the best times to experience and photograph Rocky is after a winter storm leaves the trees and mountains blanketed in glistening snow. Winter storms are often followed by bright, sunny, calm, cold days. The quiet can be deafening, as the snow absorbs ambient sounds. Consider discovering the serenity of winter months on snowshoes or cross-country skis.

BEST SUNRISE AND SUNSET SPOTS

While touring Rocky Mountain National Park in the early morning or late afternoon, you may chance upon patterns of constantly changing colors in the eastern or western sky. Multi-hued sunrises and sunsets frame the landscape, provoking awe and reflection. Here are some places with great views at dawn and day's end.

Sunset, Never Summer Range, NPS photo

Sunrise

- The best views of the sun rising are from Trail Ridge Road in the alpine tundra.
- The 360-degree view from the end of the Alpine Ridge Trail.
- Bear Lake for the breathtaking, mirror-like reflection of Hallett Peak.
- Sprague Lake and the mountain glow of the Continental Divide.
- Lily Lake with its view of Longs Peak in the soft light of morning.
- Farview Curve Overlook for the sun's reflection on the Never Summer Mountains.
- Forest Canyon Overlook to see the sunrise glow on the Continental Divide.

Sunset

- Trail Ridge Road from Forest Canyon Overlook to Medicine Bow Curve.
- Alpine Visitor Center looking east toward Mount Chapin.
- Many Parks Curve for panoramic views of Estes Park to Longs Peak.
- Evening glow of the snowcapped Mummy Range from Medicine Bow Curve.

ICONIC SUBJECTS TO PHOTOGRAPH

The perfect family snapshot at Forest Canyon Overlook. NPS photo, Ann Schonlau

If this is your first trip to Rocky Mountain National Park, you likely will be taking pictures of everything that attracts your interest. Here are some of the iconic images you may want to capture and share with your family and friends back home:

- A Rocky Mountain National Park entrance sign
- Bear Lake
- Chasm Falls
- Longs Peak from Lily Lake
- The Continental Divide sign at Milner Pass
- Sprague Lake from the north-end viewing platform
- Horseshoe Park
- The Continental Divide from Forest Canyon Overlook
- Vista from Many Parks Curve
- Mummy Range from Medicine Bow Curve
- Never Summer Mountains from Farview Curve
- Alpine Visitor Center
- Beaver Meadows Visitor Center

The best times to photograph these features are before 10 a.m. and after 4 p.m. in order to avoid deep contrasting shadows. Many professional photographers look for clear skies the morning following a cold front. You can also get great results in the early morning or late afternoon. Don't hide from stormy weather—the clouds can provide dramatic lighting.

BEST PLACES TO TAKE A PERSONAL PORTRAIT

Creating memories, Alan Leftridge

Record your visit to Rocky Mountain National Park for posterity: take a personal portrait. Most visitors look for the most memorable and iconic locations for picture backdrops. Popular spots include:

- The park entrance signs at Beaver Meadows and Grand Lake
- By the Continental Divide sign at Milner Pass
- At the shoreline of Bear Lake or Lily Lake
- The Alpine Visitor Center, when it is covered in snow

Make sure that everyone is in the photograph. You'll find plenty of fellow visitors eager to help arrange your photo.

BEST BOOKS ABOUT ROCKY

Reading about the park before you arrive will help you anticipate your experiences. Books also serve as mementos of your visit. There are numerous resources available to help you learn about the wonders of Rocky Mountain National Park. Here are some of the books you will find at your local bookstore or online.

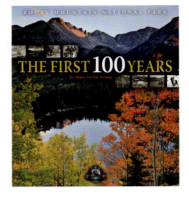

History:

- *Rocky Mountain National Park: The First 100 Years,* Mary Taylor Young
- *Enos Mills' Colorado,* James H. Pickering
- *Rocky Mountain National Park: A History,* C. W. Buchholtz
- *Making Rocky Mountain National Park: The Environmental History of an American Treasure,* Jerry J. Frank
- *A Lady's Life in the Rocky Mountains,* Isabella Bird
- *Rocky Mountain Rustic: Historic Buildings of the Rocky Mountain National Park Area,* James Lindberg, Patricia Raney, Janet Robertson

Photography:

- *A Year in Pictures: Rocky Mountain National Park,* David Dahms
- *Images of Rocky Mountain National Park,* Erik Stensland
- *Rocky Mountain National Park Impressions,* Glenn Randall
- *A Fly Fishing Guide to Rocky Mountain National Park,* Steven B. Schweitzer
- *Rocky Mountain Mammals: A Handbook of Mammals of Rocky Mountain National Park and Vicinity,* David M. Armstrong

Guidebooks:
- *A Day in Rocky*, Rocky Mountain Conservancy
- *Outdoor Family Guide to Rocky Mountain National Park*, Lisa Gollins Evans
- *Alpine Wildflowers of the Rocky Mountains*, Bettie E. Willard and Michael T. Smithson
- *Rocky Mountain: A Visitor's Companion*, George Wuerthner and Douglas W. Moore
- *Scats and Tracks of the Rocky Mountains*, James C. Halfpenny
- *Field Guide to Wildlife Viewing in Rocky Mountain National Park*, Wendy Smith
- *Rocky Mountain Wildflowers Pocket Guide*, David Dahms
- *Rocky Mountain Tree Finder*, Tom Watts & Bridget Watts
- *Mammals: Wild & Watchable Wildlife*, Rocky Mountain Conservancy
- *Geology along Trail Ridge Road: A Self-Guided Tour for Motorists*, Omer B. Raup

Hiking:
- *Rocky Mountain National Park: The Complete Hiking Guide*, Lisa Foster
- *Best Easy Day Hikes Rocky Mountain National Park*, Kent Dannen

Kids' Books:
- *Black Bear Babies!*, Donald M. Jones
- *If You Were a Bear*, Rachel Mazur
- *Who Pooped in the Park? Rocky Mountain National Park*, Gary Robson
- *Cimarron the Bighorn Sheep*, Sylvester Allred
- *Nature Trails in the Woods*, Maurice Pledger

Essential Pamphlets:

The Rocky Mountain Conservancy offers several site-specific pamphlets. You can acquire them before your visit by contacting the Conservancy online at rmconservancy.org, or at one of the visitor centers as you enter the park.

- *Guide to the Moraine Park Visitor Center & Interpretive Trail*
- *Guide to Trail Ridge Road*
- *Bear Lake Nature Trail*
- *A Guide to Wild Basin: Ouzel Country*
- *Guide to Holzwarth Trout Lodge History Site*
- *Guide to Old Fall River Road*
- *Rocky Kids Explorer Newspaper*

RESOURCES

There are many ways to learn about the natural and cultural heritage of Rocky Mountain National Park and the immediate vicinity. The National Park Service and private foundations offer services and information that will enhance your visit.

Rocky Mountain National Park
Here are the official government address, website, and phone number for information about the park:
Rocky Mountain National Park
1000 Highway 36
Estes Park, CO 80517
www.nps.gov/romo
Park information line: 970.586.1206

Rocky Mountain Conservancy
The Conservancy is a nonprofit corporation, with a mission to support *stewardship of Rocky Mountain National Park and similar lands through education and philanthropy*. The Conservancy develops informational brochures, supports educational programs, and facilitates research projects in the park. Its Field Institute presents a series of seminars and workshops covering natural history and cultural heritage topics. The member organization also administers a Conservation Corps, oversees education and research fellowships, and operates a conference facility.
www.RMConservancy.org

Rockymountainnationalpark.com
This is a commercial website for things to do, where to stay, getting around, planning your trip, trails and maps, and ways to explore the area.
http://rockymountainnationalpark.com

Rocky Mountain National Park – RMNP
This website has up-to-date information on planning your visit, fauna, flora, Estes Park lodging, and interesting things to do.
http://rmnp.com

National Park Foundation
The Foundation is a national charitable nonprofit that through philanthropy, outreach, and partnering supports the mission of the National Park Service to protect its lands for future generations.
www.nationalparks.org/explore-parks/rocky-mountain-national-park

US-Parks
The website is a trip planning guide for national parks and scenic highways. You can book hotels, find activities, and read about local plants, animals, and geology.
www.us-parks.com/rocky-mountain-national-park/rocky-mountain-national-park.html

National Parks Conservation Association
The mission of the National Parks Conservation Association is *to protect and enhance America's National Park System for present and future generations.* NPCA is a member organization focused on protecting the National Park System.
www.npca.org

Emerald Lake, NPS photo, Ann Schonlau

ABOUT THE AUTHOR

    Alan Leftridge first visited Rocky Mountain National Park with his family when he was eight. The Rockies revealed wonders that were emblazoned in his memory, and were instrumental in focusing him on a life-long pathway. Since that first experience, he has returned to Rocky often to discover more of its secrets.

    Inspired by his visits to the park, Alan earned a biology degree at the University of Central Missouri, a secondary teaching credential from the University of Montana, and a Ph.D. in science education at Kansas State University.

    Alan's enthusiasm for the outdoors led him to work as a seasonal park naturalist and a wilderness ranger. He taught high school science, environmental education at Miami University, and environmental studies at Humboldt State University. He continues to advance the art of interpretive writing through seminars for organizations and government agencies worldwide. His books include The Best of Yellowstone National Park, The Best of Glacier National Park, Glacier Day Hikes, Seeley-Swan Day Hikes, Going to Glacier, and Interpretive Writing. Alan lives in the Swan Valley of northwestern Montana.